BITCOIN
GUIDE BOOK FOR BEGINNERS

2 Books in 1

Bitcoin Blueprint & Invest in Digital Gold

Wallets, Bitcoin ATM-s, Bitcoin mining, Investing &Trading

by
Keizer Söze

Copyright

All rights reserved. No part of this book may be reproduced in any form or by any electronic, print or mechanical means, including information storage and retrieval systems, without permission in writing from the publisher.

Copyright © 2017 Keizer Söze

Disclaimer

This Book is produced with the goal of providing information that is as accurate and reliable as possible. Regardless, purchasing this Book can be seen as consent to the fact that both the publisher and the author of this book are in no way experts on the topics discussed within and that any recommendations or suggestions that are made herein are for entertainment purposes only.

Professionals should be consulted as needed before undertaking any of the action endorsed herein.
Under no circumstances will any legal responsibility or blame be held against the publisher for any reparation, damages, or monetary loss due to the information herein, either directly or indirectly.

This declaration is deemed fair and valid by both the American Bar Association and the Committee of Publishers Association and is legally binding throughout the United States.

The information in the following pages is broadly considered to be a truthful and accurate account of facts and as such any inattention, use or misuse of the information in question by the reader will render any resulting actions solely under their purview.

There are no scenarios in which the publisher or the original author of this work can be in any fashion deemed liable for any hardship or damages that may befall the reader or anyone else after undertaking information described herein.

Additionally, the information in the following pages is intended only for informational purposes and should thus be thought of as universal.

As befitting its nature, it is presented without assurance regarding its prolonged validity or interim quality. Trademarks that are mentioned are done without written consent and can in no way be considered an endorsement from the trademark holder.

Table of Contents – Book 1

Chapter 1 - Digital Gold………………………..12

Chapter 2 - Early Investors…………………...20

Chapter 3 - Competition……………………...26

Chapter 4 - Bitcoin in the born………………30

Chapter 5 - The man with the plan……………35

Chapter 6 - Bitcoin is the FUTURE!....................41

Chapter 7 - Fiat Currency VS Bitcoin…………48

Chapter 8 - Bitcoin VS Gold…………………..53

Chapter 9 - Dept Payments ………………….57

Chapter 10 - The power of uniqueness ………..60

Chapter 11 - Bitcoin in a recruit………………..66

Chapter 12 - Mining process of Bitcoin………..71

Chapter 13 - Bitcoin evolution…………………76

Chapter 14 - Purchase Power………………...84

Chapter 15 - Get ready for the revolution……..89

Table of Contents – Book 2

Chapter 1 - Why consider Bitcoin……………144

Chapter 2 – Peer-to-Peer Economy……………123

Chapter 3 - Is Bitcoin dead?................................127

Chapter 4 - Will Bitcoin hit $1million?.............131

Chapter 5 – Are you late for Bitcoin?................136

Chapter 6 – 11 Reasons to invest in Bitcoin….140

Chapter 7 – Potential risk of Bitcoin………….146

Chapter 8 – LocalBitcoins…………………..152

Chapter 9 – Hot wallets………………………..156

Chapter 10 – Cold wallets……………………..162

Chapter 11 – Wallet recommendation………..169

Chapter 12 – Bitcoin ATM-s…………………..182

Chapter 13 – Best Online Trading platforms...189

Chapter 14 - Be aware of scammers!..................203

Chapter 15 – Bitcoin Trading…………………..216

BITCOIN

Blueprint

Volume 1

by
Keizer Söze

Introduction

Congratulations on purchasing this book and thank you for doing so.

This book is an excellent beginner's guide to understand Bitcoin. The contents avoid technical details to provide better understanding to those are new to this technology. There are certain terms that some technical background in Information Technology would help, however, it's not necessary. Everyday english has been used through this book to avoid confusion. This book will take you by the hand to show you, step-by-step, how digital currency was born. For better understanding, first, it begins with a brief introduction of Bitcoin and why often called as Digital Gold. Furthermore, it takes a look at why people are sceptical when it comes to Bitcoin, by analyzing the current market. Next, we take a look at some examples of key individuals, who had an opportunity of getting know Bitcoin at its early days. Followed by explaining the differences between gambling and investing, with the method of understanding some of the key features of Bitcoin technology.

Next, introducing ,,the man with the plan" aka the inventor of Bitcoin. Next, we comapare Bitcoin to Fiat Currencies, as well precious metals such as gold, and understand the facts why Bitcoin is so powerful. Once uniqueness of Bitcoin has explained, we exhibit the possibilities of how it can save us from the Dept that inflation has created by old fashioned currencies.

Next, we take a look at how Bitcoin is recruiting the miners, as well what key responsibilities the miners have, and how Bitcoin mining process has been established. Followed by, understand the current market trend, and where Bitcoin already in use, and what are the future plans for further expansion.

In the bonus chapter, we'll go into more detail on how you can get paid in Bitcoin, using Blockchain technology, and how it is extremely beneficial for future of payroll. Finishing by understanding the future of recruitment process, and reputation system that Bitcoin – Blockchain technology can, and already providing us.

There are plenty of books on this subject in the market, thanks again for choosing this one! Every effort was made to ensure the book is riddled with as much useful information as possible. Please enjoy!

Chapter 1 - Digital Gold

So, you probably heard about Bitcoin, and now thinking to learn more about it. Perhaps, you don't even want to tell your friends or family, only just want to know more about it.

You may be thinking to keep this in secret, and not to talk about it. Some of your friends would laugh at you because you spend your time learning about such thing as Bitcoin.

Some of your relatives would look at you like you are an alien, especially when you mention words like Bitcoin, the blockchain, or cryptocurrency? Some people you know, may tell you things like:,,yeah yeah whatever, I don't care, it's nonsense!,, Some of your friends may act as they care, but, continuously asking questions that have negativity about Bitcoin.

When you ask your friends or relatives and their opinion about investing in Bitcoin, they have no clue what to say, perhaps want to talk you out of it? Do you have a feeling when you talk about Bitcoin to your closed ones, most of them thinking that you are crazy?

In case any of the above mentioned is familiar to you, then don't worry. It's completely normal. The reality is that most people have no clue about the power of Bitcoin, or even what it is. Bitcoin is in the media here and there, mostly, when hackers hit large companies, using techniques like Ransomware, then asking for ransom pain in Bitcoin.

Another famous news, is when Bitcoin is related to terrorists, pornography, drug dealers, arms dealers or some business that's on the dark web, and the only way to pay for those are using Bitcoin. Either way, it is hard to believe that some people never heard of Bitcoin, yet from my experience, it is not exactly correct. Anyhow I have experienced them all, and most responses from people are:

,,I didn't have time to check what is Bitcoin,, or

,,I am too dumb to understand it,, but the best ones are:
,, You should keep this subject to your nerd friends, because I don't care,,

Of course, I have all sort of friends, both investors, as well traders. However, it wasn't always like that, especially when first time I heard of Bitcoin.

Also realized, for some reason people don't talk about it. One of the reasons could be people might hide something, and only want to use this cryptocurrency for bad intentions. I might be wrong. However, the main reason people don't talk about Bitcoin is they don't know what it is, how it works, how to buy, how to spend, how to keep it securely, and so on.

One of my best friends has never heard of Bitcoin or blockchain until I told him. However he is my best friend and all, still just recently said that he doesn't know what will be the outcome. Obviously, he has still no clue what's going on, and that's fine.

My brother has some arguments about Bitcoin, however, when I explained how Blockchain works, which is the platform that allows Bitcoin to run, he has changed his mind, yet still scared of becoming an investor.

My Father has taken keen interests, however, he is very similar to me, and first want to understand how the underlying technology works before he would invest, and this is great!

Another friend of mine is super excited about the idea of investing in Bitcoin. However, he believes the security is number one priority, and he is currently waiting for a Cryptocurrency hardware wallet. He is ordering Ledger Nano.

However, they are completely running out of stock, and the earliest they can deliver is eight weeks ahead. He has decided to learn everything there is to know about Bitcoin in the mean while waiting for the wallet. My opinion on that, he has made the right choice, and it is a wise move.

I will get into wallets, sizes, prices, where to order from, what are the differences, however for now let me introduce Bitcoin, and its glory.

This book is written in August 2017. Therefore if you read it the future, the Market capitalization will be not the same. However right now the Market capitalization of the Bitcoin is $47,679,723,632, and the current price of Bitcoin, against the dollar, is $2891.79

If you ask me on the amount of; 47 Billion dollar +, and still counting? Yes, it's a lot of money that has been invested into Bitcoin alone.

But, why would anyone ever buy Bitcoin? There are multiple answers to that. However, mostly investors, and investing are about building our portfolio.

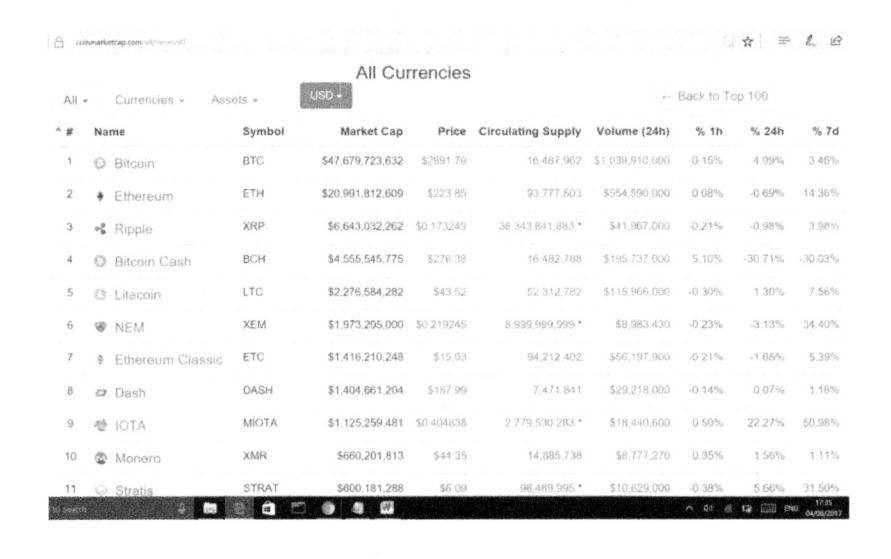

Note: The screenshot above has been taken on the 4th of August 2017, and the source is www.coinmarketcap.com

Why is it a good investment?

Well, let's look at the quick history of Bitcoin, and its value. I am using the same source from coinmarketcap.com, however, this time I click on Bitcoin to see more details.

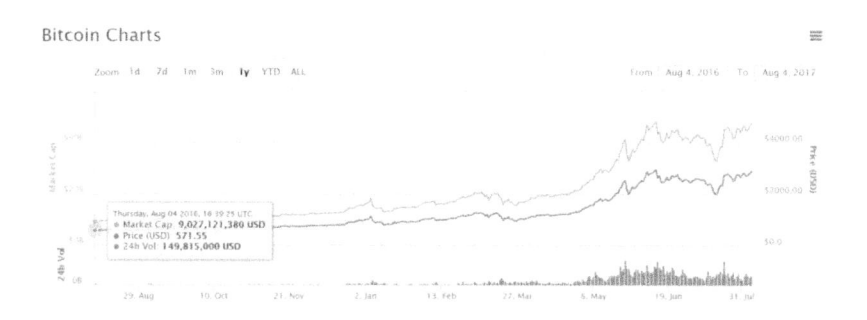

Next, clicking on 1Y on the Zoom field, and now the Bitcoin chart shows me the details of year to date prices. As you can see, exactly a year ago, on 4th of August 2016, the market Capitalization was only $9,027,121,380 billion dollars, however, to round up this figure, let's just say 9 Billion dollars.

If I have to compare this number to the current 47 billion dollars, I could round it up again by saying, only within the last year the market capitalization has became five times more than it was.

In the same time, the value of one Bitcoin was 571.55 dollars. Taking this figure further, I have calculated how much Bitcoin has increased in value over the last year. So again, what I have done is simple; divid 2891.79 by 571.55, and I got an outcome of 5.059. I will round it up to five for better illustration.

However, I believe you can see that the value has increased five times within last year. This means 500% profit. There is no bank I know of, that is capable of doing that, however, if you do know one, please let me know.

Unfortunately coinmarketcap.com is only shows data since 2013, however, another excellent resource in the Crypto world is www.conindesk.com Navigating to coindesk.com, I would like to share with you the value of Bitcoin since it's inception. Unfortunately, even coindesk.com shows only the Bitcoin data since 2010, however, that should be just good enough for the purpose of what I am about to show you.

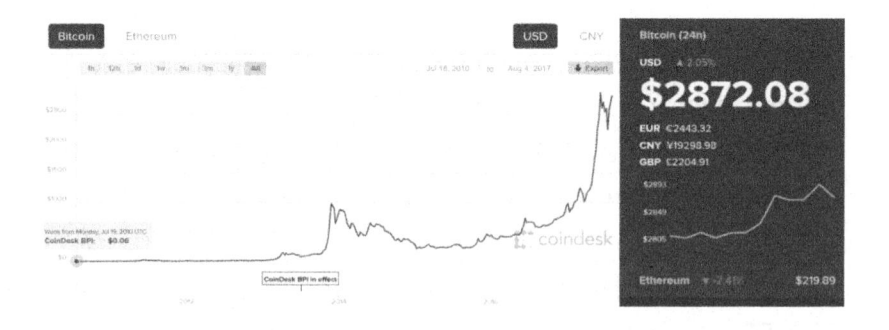

You can see that on the 19th of July 2010, Bitcoin was worth 0.06 dollars. Seven years has past since, and having a quick calculation; you should see that the value has not only five times but 47,868 times has been grown since.

So basically if you would have bought Bitcoin in 2010, for 100 dollars, today it would worth of $4,7 million dollars.

Chapter 2 – Early Investors

Roger Ver aka Bitcoin Jesus

There are many people who have participated purchasing Bitcoin back in the day. They are known as early investors, and today, they are known as Crypto-millionaires. One, that is the most famous worth to mention: called Roger Ver, also known as Bitcoin Jesus.

In 2011, Bitcoin has begun to grow in value, and reached 1 dollar. It was a turning point for many people, and Roger started to learn about Bitcoin and the technology behind called Blockchain. At the same time, he was so convinced that Bitcoin is a Digital Gold, that he has begun to invest. Roger had invested 25,000 dollars into Bitcoin when the price was around 1 dollar. He has deployed some of it, however, even he kept half of it't Bicoin, still that could possibly worth around 35-50 millions of dollars. Roger has multiple companies, as well many start-ups, where he has invested heavily over the years.

All though, some of his involvements are not always favour of everyone in a Bitcoin community, Roger gets into trouble by people misunderstanding his intentions.

Some believe that Satoshi Nakamoto had a different plan, such as the Bitcoin should be completely decentralized, however, Roger also got involved in some Cryprocurrencies where the intentions are to centralize some of those crypto coins.

What people seem to misunderstand, is that Roger is not Jesus, but a business man. Again this is what some people just can't understand, therefore Roger has been called Bitcoin Anticryst too.

Anyhow, Roger is mainly known for a title of Bitcoin Jesus, and I wanted you to know by introducing him, as once you will get involved more in the playground of Bitcoin, his name will keep on coming up from different sources again, and again.

Winklevoss Brothers

Yes, they have some involvements to Facebook, even till today, however, they also have a few involvements in Cryptocurrencies, as well Bitcoin.

In 2012, they met a friend who had a friend of another friend who has introduced them the idea of Digital Currency. Cameron has been interested, and began to learn about it. Next he has quickly have presented the idea to his brother Tyler.

Together, they have came to the conclusion that Bitcoin is either a bogus or something big that will change the world. Around 2012, the value of Bitcoin was around 100 dollars when they began to invest slowly. One thing lead to another, they have started to invest heavily, and by the end of the year, they were able to buy up 1% of all Bitcoin in circulation. At the time they have invested around $11 million dollars buying Bitcoin, however, that value has grown at least 25-30 times by today. In US dollar today 2017 they have as much Bitcoin that worth between $275 million to $300 million dollars.

Steve's story

There are just too many people who have become wealthy. However, there are also speculations around Bitcoin. For example one of my friends, Steve, just recently told me his story what happened back in 2013.

Steve has never believed in Bitcoin until it reached the value of $100. But then suddenly Bitcoin went crazy, and the value has changed to $200.

So, he said he was going to wait for the right moment to invest, and it meant for him that once Bitcoin goes back to $100, he will invest for $10,000 dollars worth. He has kept on waiting, and waiting then suddenly the value of Bitcoin has changed from $200 to 300 dollars.

He didn't know what to do, if he should wait or not, so he has invested into Bitcoin, buying 10 Bitcoin for

3000 dollars in November 2013. However in the same month, Bitcoin has reached $900, and he has sold all his Bitcoin. Steve has made a good profit, however, he told me recently that he was very lucky.

I told him that those Bitcoin would worth lots more now, and if he would have kept on hold of it, he could have a better portfolio, however he couldn't care less.

Gambling vs. investing

The reality, is there are many early investors, and there are plenty of success stories around these people, yet some may call them early gamblers.

The fact is that no one knows what the future brings. However, people do their best, and those not afraid, will succeed. I have learned it for a while now, and it is easier than you think.

To overcome fear, one of the best solution, is to be confident. There is no point to be confident in a decision that you have not done any research on, therefore it is always vital to understand what exactly you invest into. Again, it's a straightforward process. Do your research, learn as much as you can until you have no doubt. In order to reach that point, you will know what you have to do.

Believe me, it can go in two ways, either you are confident what you know through the process of continuous learning, or you are confident that the particular project doesn't make you confident enough to invest, and move on to another project.

Chapter 3 – Competition

The reality is, that in 2015 to 2016 Bitcoin had less value, and pretty much was moving on the scale of between $300 - 600 dollars. However, in those two years, there were many other cryptocurrencies born, in fact, hundreds of other cryptocurrencies arrived to the Crypto market to compete with Bitcoin.

So far no luck for any other cryptocurrencies to beat Bitcoin, and by navigating back to coinmarketcap.com, as of today, there are 1032 other currencies exist. As you can see I have included in the screenshot the date; 4th of August 2017. Those who think that one or two other cryptocurrencies can take over Bitcoin, I think it's pretty evident that for nine years, thousand + currencies just couldn't succeed.

Not only couldn't do it, but Bitcoin became even stronger in value, in fact, the highest of them all. These are simple facts, and even bad reputation by criminal usage, or hundreds of fake news, just can not change. Bitcoin does not care what's in the news, or what people opinion is; it looks after itself, makes corrections, and so far it seems, the sky is the limit.

The beauty of making a profit on Bitcoin, is there is no tax to pay. There is no company called Bitcoin, and there is no server called Bitcoin, neither Bank called Bitcoin.

Bitcoin is running on a completely decentralized peer-to-peer network, where, there is no master node or primary server, therefore there is no boss. It's running on a technology called blockchain, where, in every 10 minutes, there is a new block get's validated by proof of work, using mathematical computation power, using very sophisticated Cryptography known as Elliptic Curve.

Bitcoin's algorithm also includes the discrete logarithm problem, that not only provides one of the best security in the world, but creating an un-hackable system.

Note: More detailed guide on Block creation, can be found in the Blockchain books, particularly technical guide in Volume 2 – Mastering Blockchain.

What you have to understand is that Bitcoin is here to stay, and not going anywhere. It is unstoppable, therefore people, governments, banks or financial institutions, like it or not.

You might have heard the sentence sounds like this: ,, If you can't beat them, you have to join them.,,

Well, that is what exactly banks do now. Not only investing heavily to Cryptocurrencies like Bitcoin or Ethereum, but creating their digital currencies.

One of the most famous called: Ripple. Ripple is already on the market with the current capitalization of $6.6 Billion being on the third place.

#	Name	Symbol	Market Cap	Price	Circulating Supply	Volume (24h)	% 1h	% 24h	% 7d
1	Bitcoin	BTC	$47,082,505,533	$2856.51	16,488,300	$1,020,570,000	-0.45%	3.46%	2.09%
2	Ethereum	ETH	$20,926,889,819	$223.15	93,780,736	$551,985,000	0.31%	-0.88%	14.31%
3	Ripple	XRP	$6,653,960,257	$0.173534	38,343,841,883	$45,507,700	-0.15%	-0.82%	4.27%

You have to ask the question: Are they scared of Bitcoin? Or they just see that it's an excellent opportunity for them too?

It is indeed a wonderful opportunity for everyone. No matter who you are, an individual, a bank, a criminal, it works for everyone.

Chapter 4 – Bitcoin in the born

So, why Bitcoin? There are many other cryptocurrencies on the market, however, for some reason, Bitcoin seems to be the winner of all. The answer might be simpler than you think. It is the most wildly implemented Cryptocurrency, and the reality is that most people look at cryptocurrency, as Bitcoin only. I have some many friends who never heard of any other cryptocurrency except for Bitcoin. People just never heard of other currencies, however most of them did hear about Bitcoin.

Furthermore, I already touched on the dark web, and Bitcoin is what everyone accepts on there, however it the other hand, accepting Bitcoin has been legalized in many countries recently. In Japan, it's been announced, that by the end of Summer 2017, there will be 260,000 Stores that will accept Bitcoin as a paying method.

Along with Japan, there is another major country Russia, who also looking at legalizing Bitcoin as a legal paying method. I love the idea of choice: cash, card, or crypto, when you about to pay in the supermarket. As there are more and more countries becoming interested in the idea of Bitcoin Payment, the rest of the world will catch up too.

Before we get into more detailed facts, let's understand how the idea has developed over the years, until we reached to implement Bitcoin.

In the 1970's there was a lot of interests in Cryptography, especially in how mathematical algorithms can change the world, by using it as money, or at least, as part of a payment method. Diffie Hellman Key Exchange was very promising, in fact, we still use the same methods for our current online banking for security.

Note: Diffie Hallmen Key exchange explained in my previous Book: Mastering Blockchain - Volume 2

Unfortunately, when it comes to digital data transfer, a new problem has been introduced, that is known as double spending. Just think of it like I have a digital photo that I am emailing you. What happens is we now both having the same image, unless I delete it. However, you would never find out if I ever did delete it. Then you could easily send the same image to some of your friends or family members; therefore we could easily duplicate digital data, and we still are. However double spending problem has been resolved over the years, and now it has it's own platform. Running as an application in a software form, on the top of the internet, and the technology called Blockchain.

Double spending problem
Double spending problem is the main issue that needed to be solved to introduce a new electronic money system. The problem could have been solved by using a central trusted third party online, that could verify the electronic cash has not been spent yet.

Back in the day, the idea was that this trusted third party could have been anyone like a bank, broker, or any entity, someone who can facilitate interactions between two sides. Anyone, however the problem was that trust the third party, would be still required. Of course, there are plenty of disadvantages for trusting in third parties, in fact in any financial services.

In 2008, when financial crisis hit, several banks failed, taught us, there is no such thing as trusted third party. They have failed mainly because of mismanagement, greed, or even because of involvement of illegal bank activities. Furthermore, half of the adults around the world have no access to financial services, because financial institutions are too far away or too expensive to use. Third parties are commercial entities; therefore, they will charge fees for their services.

If you think about inventing a new electronic money, one of your goals should be to make it accessible to anyone around the world. Third parties have the power to suspend customers accounts. For example, a few years ago PayPal has suspended WikiLeaks donation account, and froze its assets.

PayPal claimed, WikiLeaks to encourage others to engage in illegal activity. This was not a result of legal process but rather, the result of fear of falling out of the favor with Washington. Third parties can also deny or limit access to your assets. For example in 2015, the in Greece, the banks have limited access for cash withdrawal because of the rush on the banks.

Double spending solution
The solution for double spending without third party now exist, and that is what blockchain allowed for Bitcoin. Bitcoin was the first application which has solved the double spending problem without

the use of third parties, or having any involvement with any centralized system. Satoshi Nakamoto has came up with an idea of Bitcoin, and created its original reference implementation.

Satoshi has solved the double spending problem, using a technology called Blockchain. The system is based on cryptographic proof, instead of trust. Blockchain technology was originally used as a cryptocurrency for the payment transaction between two parties, but nowadays it can be used many other services such as:

- Notary Services,
- Identity services,
- Voting services, and so on

Chapter 5 – The man with the plan

Note: I have explained in great details regards to Satoshi Nakamoto and multiple theories as well facts around the real inventor in my book called: Blockchain for beginners Volume 1.

I have dedicated four chapters around Satoshi Nakamoto, in Volume starting from Chapter 5 to Chapter 8, however if you have not that book yet, I will provide a little overview of who Satoshi Nakamoto is. In case you have read my book Blockchain for beginners, you may skip to the next chapter now.

Satoshi Nakamoto

First, I would like you to understand that this book has been written in the second quarter of 2017. Therefore, by the time you are reading this book, it's possible that new light might be shed on who Satoshi Nakamoto is.

With the current knowledge at hand, let's try to understand who Satoshi Nakamoto is.

First of all, Satoshi Nakamoto is an inventor of Bitcoin, as well the blockchain technology. All through it's a false name, this is how he introduced himself to the internet. It is a men's name.

However, it is possible the Satoshi Nakamoto might be a woman. This is one of the biggest mysteries in the technology world. Yet, most people don't want to know exactly who Satoshi is; nevertheless, they are thankful for the technology he created.

Unfortunately, many people think that because Satoshi Nakamoto has invented Bitcoin and the blockchain technology, he is also the owner of those too. The reality is that Satoshi Nakamoto has no control over the Blockchain—neither bitcoin; therefore, it really doesn't matter who Satoshi Nakamoto is.

But yeah, we still want to know who is behind the curtains; so, let's think about it again. Satoshi Nakamoto is reasonably a man or a woman—of course—he could be a couple, a group of people, or even a group of women for all we know. Satoshi Nakamoto might be ten people together, but also could be a massive team of 100 individuals.

Satoshi Nakamoto might be a child, or he could be old men. Satoshi Nakamoto might have died right after he released his white paper; therefore, he had no time to show his real face.

I do understand if you are getting bored of these accusations, so let's begin thinking in a different perspective. Satoshi Nakamoto might not even be human. Well, you might think of me being over the limit.

However, it's just so odd that we couldn't figure out who Satoshi Nakamoto is in the past decade; not where he resided, but who he is—honestly—we have no idea. Someone might know exactly who he is. However, there is no confirmation that would ever have enough evidence to prove who Satoshi is.

I've always loved to watch sci-fi movies, and I came across one called Arrival. Some of these super old movies, still hold up today. For example, back in the day, some sci-fi stories featured individual objects, or tools that we might use in the future and some that we've already been using for years. I don't want to get into too many specifics; however, think about face time talk back in the 80's. It was a concept that one day we might be able to do that.

And nowadays Skype and Facebook Video Chat is in our daily lives. In fact, there are millions of people connected and capable of being on skype video chat for hours, using our cell phones. The first iPhone was created and launched to the market ten years ago, in 2007. Since we have gone through some dramatic changes, and the next decade will be even more impressive.

So back to the picture called Arrival, I hope that you have seen it already too, and that I will not spoil it for you. However, if you haven't seen it yet, you might want to skip the next few lines.

In the movie, we have received a visit from Aliens that are here to help us by providing visibility in the future. Again, sorry if you have not watched the movie yet, you will probably hate me for this. The concepts of the film are excellent, no wonder it received an Oscar, even though it might have deserved more than that, but that's just my opinion.

When I think about this sci-fi movie, I am thinking about the fact that it is very similar to the same concepts.

We have received a technology called Blockchain from an unknown person—or I should say from an anonymous source—that will change our world dramatically! I wonder how the film creators came across the idea...

I am not suggesting that there are Aliens out there, but I can't deny it either. What I can tell you is that IT Professionals, Software Developers, Experience Programmers, even Cybersecurity Experts are fascinated by this technology, and often refer to it as an ALIAN TECHNOLOGY."

The blockchain is huge, and it certainly takes months, if not years, to fully understand it's technical details, and how it fits together.

Another thing is that, more and more often, it is said that this technology is just too complex for one man to build. Therefore, there is no way that Satoshi Nakamoto was working on it alone.

So back to the million-dollar question, "Who is Satoshi Nakamoto?"

Let's look at some of the claims over the years so that you can decide for yourself.

What you have to understand is that Satoshi Nakamoto went silent in 2009, and remained like that for the next five years, or at least on the forum where he previously posted and was always active.

Note: For further reading on Satoshi Nakamoto, please visit the book called Blockchain for Beginners – Volume 1.

Chapter 6 – Bitcoin is the FUTURE

Many friends often ask me:
Keizer! – How can you define in simple terms what Bitcoin is?

Well, the answer always depends on who asked the question. If you are completely new to Bitcoin, like I was at first, I even thought at some point that Bitcoin has a physical form. However, Bitcoin is completely virtualized, therefore untouchable. Now that you have a bit of understanding who Satoshi Nakamoto is, you must know that he has created a software called Blockchain; however, the intention of the software was to introduce an application. To run the application, it was required to be run on a network, that is known as a peer-to-peer network.

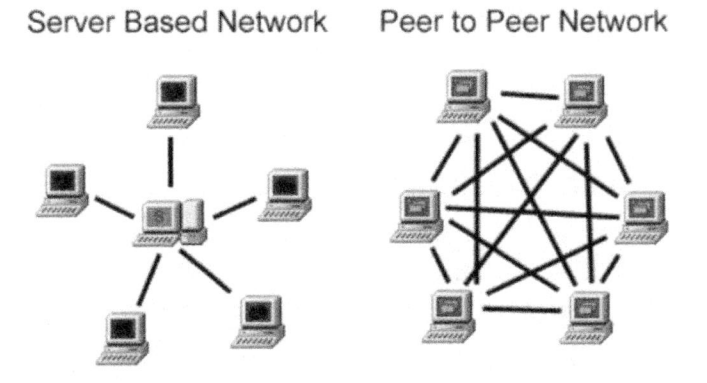

The peer-to-peer network, therefore, has created a system, and it was able to execute the application on the software.

That application's primary purpose is to introduce a new paying method, known as digital currency. Because the application is running on a peer-to-peer network, this is also known as a decentralized network or decentralized system, or I should say the best description for it: decentralized currency.

Because each transaction is required validation through proof or work, it needs to be recorded in the ledger. Therefore it's also known as a decentralized ledger system.

A currency that has no centralized system, it can not be tempered, therefore providing a single source of truth. A single source of truth that is validated by proof of work, therefore it's a technology.

In fact, Bitcoin is running on multiple algorithms, and protocols using the internet, therefore it's a combined into a very sophisticated technology.

Because it's using combined technology, it can't be manipulated. The peer-to-peer network requires internet access, and because it's running on the web, I could also say: it is the currency of the internet. Because nobody owns it, and there is no Bitcoin boss, I could also say that is the money of the people. Sure, the banks can invest too.

However it's not owned by them, and they can not lend it, well at least not yet. Bitcoin account does not require to provide your name, address, race, age, occupation, all there is necessary to have internet access. It is capable of providing anonymity, so I could also call it: Anonymous payment system.

So back to our question: what is Bitcoin? Well, Bitcoin is representing our future, in fact, the future of money, as the transactions will not require banks or any trusted third party, therefore it's not only excellent, but the best solution to do business in the future. Let's look at Bitcoin in a bit more detail.

Bitcoin is a software

Well, Bitocin is certainly not hardware. Bitcoin network can be downloaded, and it can run on any computer, that has a connection to the internet. However, it is software.

Bitcoin is an Application

As I mentioned Bitcoin is software; however, it's running on the technology called Blockchain.

Blockchain already has thousands of other cryptocurrencies running; therefore Bitcoin itself is just one of those many applications. It is fair to mention that Bitcoin was the first application on the blockchain, and many other applications are only trying to copy or compete with Bitcoin.

Bitcoin is a network

As I mentioned before, Bitcoin is running on a peer-to-peer network. Any computer in the world can participate in the network, as there is no master node or master server. The validation process is running on every node that is part of the system once a new block gets created and added to the Blockchain.

Bitcoin is a system

Because it's running on the peer-peer network, and using multiple known technologies, it's also known as a system.

Bitcoin is money

I think you will agree with this right away. Bitcoin is the most wildly implemented and accepted cryptocurrency in the world.

Bitcoin is a decentralized Cryptocurrency

There are many more decentralized cryptocurrencies, however, again, it is fair to mention that Bitcoin was the first of them all.

Bitcoin is a decentralized ledger system.

Each transaction is required to have a validation process, as well making sure that each validation is secured in the great ledger; therefore it's also known as a decentralized ledger system.

Bitcoin is a very complex technology

Bitcoin is running Elliptic Curve Cryptography to participate in a discrete logarithm problem, also using hashing as well ASCII encoding, and many more technologies combined. The reality is that 90% of Bitcoin investors have no clue how Bitcoin works, however they know that is just working fine. If you learn how the underlying technology works, called Blockchain, you will understand why it will change the world.

Many people believe to know what Bitcoin is, however when it comes to the block validation process, as well who receives what amount of transaction fees, and on what algorithm is determining these methods, you would be surprised that very few people understand how Bitcoin really works.

Note: Further learning on Blockchain attributes and how Bitcoin works in depth, please visit my other book called: Mastering Blockchain – Advanced Guide: Volume 2

So back to the main question: What Bitcoin is in simple terms:

This is not only my opinion; however I am very confident to say that Bitcoin is the FUTURE!

It will change our lives, in fact already shaping it, and my advice to you is that faster you learn about it, sooner you understand what Bitcoin is capable, easier it will become to deal with it.

I am not only talking about investing, but learning it. There is no point to invest into anything that you do not fully understand, or at least have a high level of understanding where you put your money in the first place.

Chapter 7 – Fiat Currency VS Bitcoin

Bitcoin is so powerful, yet many people speculate around Bitcoin as well other cryptocurrencies that they are just a bubble.

The reality is that those individuals who say Bitcoin is a bubble, are mistaken. Please don't get me wrong by saying that, as I do know many people who believe that Bitcoin is a bubble, but it is only a reflection of their knowledge of Blockchain.

![Bitcoin - Innovation that disrupts]

For example my ex-boss, Andrew, who has high educations as well studying every day, well respected, not only by me, but amongst other Infrastructure, and Application Manager. Still he has not considered Blockchain enough yet, therefore he believes that Bitcoin is a bubble.

When I have explained some of the core functions, of the underlying technology called Blockchain, he has exhibited some frustrating expressions. However, after few days he was asking me about some other functions of Bitcoin, and who is behind the maintenance of the software.

Obviously, I can tell, he has changed his mind of Bitcoin since. In fact, he is consistently reminding me each time when the value of Bitcoin is going up. Before you think Bitcoin is some kind Day trading or any other easily manipulated stock market feature, I warn you now that Bitcoin has nothing to do with the Stock market.

The Stock market opens every Monday to Friday 9 am to 5 pm. Over the weekend, each nights, even weekdays the stock exchange is closed. Opposite Bitcoin is open 24/7, day and night, weekdays and weekends, there is no Bank holidays or day offs. Bitcoin as well the cryptocurrencies are running in a market that always open, and never stops. About every 10 minutes, there is a new block gets validated, and it doesn't matter what time of the day is or which country you or I reside in, new Bitcoin get's mined.

Who allowed the Bitcoin to hit the market?

This is one of those questions that many people involved and trying to figure out, but the answer is straightforward. There was nobody. There was not a single individual or company who has allowed Bitcoin to exist, in fact, there was no company been asked in the first place. Bitcoin did not ask for permission, and neither was waiting for authorization.

When the European Union together have decided to bring this new currency called: EURO, to the market, was taking years. Meetings, and long discussions on how each EURO should look like and how it should present itself in a physical form, like 5 Euro, 10 Euro, 20 Euro, and so on.

Then, a long meeting of fights and discussions, they had to decide which country is qualified to start using Euro. Next, agreements on possible printing locations, as well once Each Euro will be converted, how much it should worth according to the German Marks, or to the Italian Lira. Each country that was involved, had no choice but to participate in these long meetings of discussions around the currency, and of course many long fights too. Either way, the actual implementation has only happened in some countries according to the original plans. The point is, by the time every little detail has been discussed, the Euro already began to lose its value.

Many people have become poor after the change of currencies, and those, that had all their life time savings kept in a bank, suddenly become worthless. Of course, there was a way to making sure there is a profitable way of getting into the new currency.

However these solutions were kept for the wealthy, and those were able to make a move, which involved the right timing. Euro is a FIAT currency that was manipulated from the beginning of its existence.

It's centralized by the biggest players in Europe. In the European governments, politicians made sure that they will become rich by centralizing the Euro, however in the case of Bitcoin, there was no discussion, neither was any permission asked from those in Governments.

Bitcoin didn't ask for permission, didn't talk to the banks, neither to any politicians, in fact, most of them don't even understand how Bitcoin works. As always, when people don't know something, they don't like it, they hate it, they afraid of it, and slowly, once they understand it, they will respect it, and they will eventually invest in it.

Why I choose Bitcoin?

The reality is that Bitcoin might be spelled out in the news as fake money or bubble, however, the reality is that Bitcoin can be expanded dramatically. What I mean is Bitcoin can be easily divided into multiple fractions, while paper money is only causing issues.

For example, imagine that you have to pay for something that only costs 3 dollars in the shop, but you only have a $20 note and the shop owner does not have a change.

When it comes to Bitcoin, it is not a problem, as you can pay as much as you want, and the software will tell you exactly how much Bitcoin is 3 dollars, at the time of the payment.

Chapter 8 – Bitcoin VS Gold

Again, when it comes to payments, using gold, or any other precious metal, there is a little problem.

There are multiple challenges, so let's think about the storage first. Let's say that I would like to buy a new sofa in the shop, and I know that the price of the couch is 1kg of gold exactly.

Bitcoin VS. *Gold*

Should I take that 1kg of gold into the trunk of my car? Oh no, wait, I have to buy a plane ticket for myself, wife and the kids for our annual summer holiday too.

Those tickets, + Hotel room prices will cost about 0.57 Kg of Gold, so I have to take some gold with myself too right? There is no point in getting into this any further, as Gold or any precious metals simply can not be the solution to the future of money. They are too heavy, difficult to cut them, and the value of products are just a pain to be measured.

It would not work, and it was one of many issues why it was stopped as a paying method in the first place.

Content type?

When you think about Music, they used to be in cassette format, then CD, eventually mp3, however for a long time now, we can stream music.

Video contents, are the same, as well books. Back in the day, you had to have DVD player along with DVD-s, as well the physical books had to be carried, in order to access the contents.

However, nowadays you can stream them all. So, why should I take cash everywhere with myself if we can stream it now, like in a case of Bitcoin.

Also, if I travel to another country, I have to change my dollars to euros, or British pounds, instead we could just have Bitcoin everywhere.

Bitcoin does not require bank, neither bank card, all I need is a smart phone.

A smart phone that I am able to stream music, video, books, as well money.

This is an excellent idea. Streaming money is the future like everything else has become streamable, money can to that too.

Technology changes, and we are able to develop things that was none existing a decade ago using technology.

2 decades ago, the idea of streaming any music, or any video using a smart phone was ridiculous, and of course unbelievable.

Today, having a smartphone, all these functions can be done with no issue. Again, streaming money in the future, is not unbelievable, as we can do this already since 2008.

As a final sentence to this topic, streaming money should not be surprising to anyone, as there is nothing new to it, however commercial television and fake newspapers will try to keep this away from us, as long as possible.

Just think about like an average bank would say that they are not good enough anymore to look after your money.

Banks are always get hacked, they always take ages to get the transfers done, they are charging high fees, and they are using your money to pay their debt.

By saying such things, they should just close down right away. However, they will do their best for keep up the current system as long as possibly can.

Chapter 9 – Debt Payments

Who is paying the Debt?

Unfortunately, people still believe that only nations can issue currency. However, it's not true.

The reality is that Bitcoin has not asked for permission from any Government, neither from any bank or politician, yet exist.

Many shops already accepting Bitcoin as a paying method, however let's move on to the topic of debt.

In 2017 January, the global debt has hit the new record of $217 Trillion dollars, however since it's continuously growing. It's not only impossible to pay this amount, but this amount will not going to be paid.

So what will happen? Well, according to this figure, it seems that the sky is the limit.

So if you think that this debt can be paid back in precious metal like Gold, it is another misconception.

All the world's Gold that the Earth has, is worth all together $8.5 Trillion dollars.

That's a lot of Gold if you ask me, but let's think again, and calculate how much does all that Gold worth.

You don't have to be good in math to understand that $8.5 Trillion against $217 Trillion does not stand a chance.

So basically, if we all just donate all our Gold for the purpose of debt repayment, it would cut it.

Gold just not good enough to take over the worlds of money, in fact, can not even stand a chance.

Gold has other issues too, like storage as well transporting it from one place to another, therefore as a paying method not even worth mentioning.

Gold for Online payments, that idea, of course, is ridiculous. Lastly, in case we want to create small units for payments, Gold should not even be considered.

Chapter 10 – The power of uniqueness

I have already explained why FIAT currencies are worthless, and I am sure that you have understood it by now. In fact, everyone knows it, yet the governments are always trying to create another currency, by saying this time it will be different, but they know it will be not. Still, people have no choice, except to go with the flow and use the nation issued currency.

The good news is that we don't have to go with the flow anymore. In fact not only don't need banks anymore, but we can be our own bank. That's all nice, however, the reason that Bitcoin can take over the world of currencies, theatrically very simple, yet it's a complicated process. Bitcoin is unique, not only because it's a cryptocurrency, but Bitcoin has a limited supply. That sounds scary for some, however, let me explain a little further so you can understand it better.

Bitcoin has a limited supply of 21 million. When you think about any other FIAT currency, no one exactly knows how much money has been printed, yet when it comes to Bitcoin, there is an exact figure.

As everything else that is unique and has a limited supply, it's worth more than those products or money that has an infinite supply.

I remember when the Italians had Lira, and the notes were ranging from 1000 to 500,000.

It was ridiculous, as it was nearly worthless in the end when Euro was about to take over.

Just when the Euro has been taken over the Italian Lira, 1000 Lira was equivalent to 0.5 Euros, and the largest notes of 500,000 Lira was worth of 250 Euros. Imagine that you had 1 million Italian lira on you; however, that was only worth of 500 Euros, which is around 590 dollars.

It was silly really. Anyhow, the point is that more Lira was on the market less it was worth, and in the end, it would just become worthless. On the other hand, Bitcoin is very different.

Not only that we know exactly how much Bitcoin will be ever in the market, but we also know by when it will happen. What I mean is not all Bitcoin is currently on the market yet. Instead of flooding the market with a new currency, Bitcoin has been introduced to the market very slowly. It is depending on what year you are reading this book, however currently as of August 2017, there is only 16,499,762 Bitcoin in circulation:

I have just visited coinmarketcap.com to see exactly, however in about every 10 minutes, this figure changes. In case you want to know exactly how much Bitcoin is in circulation at the time you read this book, just visit the following link:

https://coinmarketcap.com/currencies/bitcoin/

50 Bitcoin in every 10 minutes

The exact date of the software was in 2009 3rd of January when the first 50 Bitcoin was born. Then for the next for years in every ten minutes, there was another 50 Bitcoin mined.

25 Bitcoin in every 10 minutes

From 2012 this has continued; however, the algorithm changed, and from 2012, in every ten minutes there was only 25 Bitcoin mined until 2016.

12.5 Bitcoin in every 10 minutes

Since 2016, in every 10 minutes, there is 12.5 Bitcoin is mined until 2020.

6.25 Bitcoin in every 10 minutes

From 2020, the Bitcoin algorithm will change again, and for the next four years until 2024, in every 10 minutes, there will be 6.25 Bitcoin mined.

Basically, in about every four years, the Bitcoin algorithm will change, and the amount of Bitcoin that will be mined is kept on getting halved in every four years. This process will carry on until the year of 2140. By then, there will be 21 Million Bitcoin mined, and that will be the last of Bitcoin will be ever mined.

The process of creating Bitcoin is based on Gold mining. What happens with the Gold is something very similar what is the process with the Bitcoin, however Bitcoin is based on digitally, using multiple technologies. Another similarity that Bitcoin has, is to compare it to Gold mining difficulty. There was a time when people have found lot's of Gold mines, and able to mine plenty of them, however over time, mining Gold, became more and more difficult.

As I explained previously, mining Bitcoin is getting twice as difficult in every four years; thus there will be less and less amount to be mined. When you think about this process, you might realize that it also means for each of these four year passes, the value of Bitcoin will be in a continuous increase. I am not able to predict the future, however, obviously, we all can analyze the last eight years.

Bitcoin is based on a technique of Gold mining, however, by now you must be very curious what do I mean by mining. Of course, mining also introduces another question, who the miners are?

Chapter 11 – Bitcoin in a recruit

This section will introduce who are the miners and their purpose, starting by what was the reason in the first place to create such role as a miner.

Then will move on what exactly their responsibility, and why they have a huge influence on the network.

Ending by how they participate within the mining process, and what miners must do at all times.

NOTE: This has been explained in other book called: Blockchain for beginners – Volume 1, in Chapter 10, and Chapter 11.

In case you are familiar the process of Bitcoin mining and the miner's responsibility, you may go ahead and skip the rest of this Chapter.

However, if you want to refresh your knowledge or unaware of the Bitcoin mining process you may carry on reading this chapter.

Background

Let's first think about how new value enters the system. Back in 2008, Satoshi Nakamoto only created 50,000 Bitcoin to start the process.

If you think about it, that he built all 21 million in the first place, the bitcoin would be worthless, and the idea would have been dumb. Instead, Satoshi started with a moderate amount of Bitcoin creation.

The solution

As the Bitcoin community grows, more and more value would be required for the system to be kept alive.

There is a particular process that is needed for the system to be maintained; Satoshi has come up with the solution by creating a role. This solution is not only solving one but two issues:

1. Permanently validating transactions
2. Adding new value into the existing system

The role is called: Miner.

Miners can be individuals, or any bitcoin citizen. However, over time, many large companies have been formed, such as Genesis Mining, where you, as an individual, can join and rent their mining facilities.

There are many other miners who over the years have created a pool, and many of them also offer to join these pools for certain reasons that I will discuss shortly.

The responsibility of a miner

First, let me explain why they are called miners and what it is they do. They are called miners as the analogy has been used with gold or any other precious metal.

They work together to create new value, similar to gold miners who are digging underground. However, bitcoin miners are sealing each transaction into the ledger. Therefore, we could call miners, finalizers or authenticators.

To get rewarded for such work, the miners receive bitcoins, and this is how new value is added to the system.

The miners validate, authenticate, certify, and finalize the transactions by specific processes. Once the miners have created a new block that is accepted by the citizens, the record of the transaction cannot be modified, making it permanent information. This will also become irreversible. Therefore, no one can ever challenge it or change it, in the future.

The miners are sealing the blocks, which in itself can take an enormous amount of computing power, assuring that they cannot be easily replicated. There are multiple methods that each miner may use for the validating processes.

Some of the miners may use different software, even creating their own in-house made software to speed up the authentication process. However, it doesn't matter what software they use, as all of their work will be checked.

It starts when a miner begins to gather transactions that have been broadcasted on the network, then starts checking those transactions, and eventually sealing those collections of transfers and operations into a new block.

A miner receives bitcoins as a reward for each sealed block that is added to the blockchain.

Chapter 12 – Mining process of Bitcoin

Block creation

Explaining each block creation can be done in multiple ways; however, some sound very confusing, but it also depends on how much you understand technology. Therefore, hearing or reading it the first time can be difficult to comprehend.

I already explained that miners have an unusual role for validating each transaction in the form of a block. Now, let's discuss what it takes to create each block.

1.

Start a new block. Even if the miners are halfway done validating a block, eventually, they will drop everything and concentrate on starting a new block.

2.

Select a new transaction. This is when the miners are choosing from thousands of operations that are broadcasted over the network.

3.

Check priority of the transaction. This time the miners can go back to number one by starting a new block if they find that the transaction they have selected previously is not that significant. However, if the priority is high, the miners may go on and move to the next step.

4.

Check that the transaction is valid. This is a process that every miner must check, there is no exception of avoiding this step for any miner. However, if the transaction is found to be faked, or not valid, the miners have to stop the process, and go back to number 1 and start a new block and get another, hopefully, valid transaction.

5.
Accept the transaction. If the previous transaction was tested as a valid transaction, it must be accepted.

6.
Seal the transaction. Again, if the transaction has been found valid and accepted, now it's time to seal that transaction.

7.
Add the transaction to the transaction tree inside the block. This process can only be done once all previous steps have been verified.

8.
Check for the size of transactions. The miners need to check if there are enough transactions within the transaction tree, to seal the block. If there are not enough transactions yet, the miner will not be able to seal the block until there are enough transactions. Therefore, the miners must go back to number 2 of selecting a new transaction again, and again, until there are sufficient transactions for sealing the block.

9.
Check interruptions. This is the process where the miner must make sure that no other miners have

sealed the block in the meantime with the same transactions inside the block.

10.
Seal the block. Once there are enough transactions for sealing the block, the miners will seal the block.

11.
Broadcast the block. The miners must broadcast the new block that has been sealed; however, if the miners have been interrupted within the block sealing process, they might have to start a new block all over again.

12.
Start a new block. This is the next step in the process; however, as you see, we are now back to step number 1.

As I mentioned, miners might get interrupted while they are sealing the block and once they broadcast it, if another block has already been sealed by another miner with the same transactions within a block, the block will not be accepted. Therefore, you must start a new block.

Each block is created about every 10 minutes. As a result, 144 blocks are created each day. As I mentioned before, the miners who have successfully added a new block into a blockchain get rewarded a degree of bitcoin.

The reward for each new block creation used to be 50 bitcoins from 2009 until 2012. The reward for a new block gets halved every four years; therefore, from 2012, until 2016, the award for each new block used to be 25 bitcoins.

Currently, since 2016, until 2020, the reward to a miner for a new block that is added to the blockchain is 12.5 bitcoins; however, from 2020, it will be only 6.25 bitcoins until 2024. This process will be continued until 2140 until the last bitcoin will be created.

Chapter 13 – Bitcoin evolution

The question around what Bitcoin can become is indeed what many people concerns, as well excited about. Bitcoin can stop many people's current job, and especially those are working in Banks or financial institutions.

Banks are not happy about Bitcoin, as there is a constant fear that Bitcoin can steal their job anytime shortly.

Bankers, as well stock Brokers are in fear, however, most of them getting the feeling of safety as they have begun to invest in Bitcoin, as well learn about, what Bitcoin is becoming shortly.

Its' ok to be the sceptic; however there is a limit and people should realize this by looking back to the history of recent technology that created evolution, as well a revolution of today. Yes, I am talking about the internet; however, there are other notable technologies too that I will mention in this chapter.

Internet

It stands for interconnected networks, of course, you are probably known that already. It is known for other names too such as www – aka world wide web, net or web.

At first, it was slow and painful, there is no doubt about that. However it has evolved, and there were more and more websites to visit. Still, there was a problem, you must have typed the website address into your browser to visit a particular page.

As I said it was painful, and people were sceptical that this is not going to work. Imagine if you have mistyped a website address, you got nowhere, then you had to figure out what did you do wrong.

So it wasn't making any sense, it was more like a pain to find any website, and for many people the internet wasn't just it. There was a belief that the internet will not work ever. As always, when there is a problem, some of us keep thinking about a solution. The solution was Google.com, a search engine where you can type in few words that you are interested about, and you will get related pages.

That was the first part of the evolution of the internet; however more people have begun to use the internet, more it was believed that it would not survive all that traffic.

Again, a solution was introduced, and the internet has started to scale, where internet service providers have born. Those ISP-s – Internet Service Providers have been providing additional internet routes for end users for faster connection and reliability.

Once emails were introduced and began to scale by having an increasing number of users, it was another new belief, that the internet would not be able to handle that traffic, and the e-mail system will kill the internet.

Of course, it was stabilized very quickly, however people began to attach files, and images to the e-mails, and this new type of communication seemed to be a killer of the web.

Just imagine the traffic growth on those networks where few email attachments have made the actual email size by 10, even 20 times bigger. Emails used to take a day to get it delivered; however, this issue has been overcome again, by extending the network with better and newer technology.

Once voice and video over IP (Internet Protocol) were introduced, people got so scared that they believed the web would not only can't be scaled, but it will shut down.

This was also a false prediction, as we know the world today, or at least in 2017 when this book was written. We have multiple services where we can pay a subscription, or even for free, able to stream voice and videos anytime and the quality is excellent.

One of the most famous video conferences that are freely used is Skype; however, there are much more like it, such as WhatsApp or Facebook Messenger. Once it comes to video content like Vimeo or youtube, you know that these channels just work all the time and there is no issue with the quality that the 'current ISP-s are providing.

The internet as we know today is where every large company has moved their businesses, including banks and large shops. You can buy holidays, book Hotels, shop pretty much anything anytime. As you can see the internet has changed dramatically over the last two decades, and it has completely changed our lives and the way we think.

Linux

Yes, it is an operating system that apparently not many can handle, yet let me discover you, how Linux has changed our life. Linux is a free open source software, that was created in 1991 by Linus Torvalds; however, it is based on a Unix operating system.

Unix dated back to the end of 1960-s, however it has become known only in the 90-s to the world. Linux has so many different kinds of flavours that are just endless, in fact, you can create your version of Linux due to its open source code.

However, back in the 90-s, it was known as a worthless free software, as anyone can download a copy for free and make modifications to it, had no real value.

When people hear Linux as an operating system often get scared and run away. It is a misconception and a wrong belief that Linux OS is a complicated system to handle. 2 decades later, nearly everyone has at least one Linux based device. The reality is that back in the day, Linux was the favourite operating system of all computer nerds, including me.

It had no desktop version at first; therefore anything you wanted to do, was based on the CLI – Command Line Interface.

Yes, that's right, a black screen with white letters on it. No desktop, no start menu, no visible folders, or fancy picture graphics, nothing but a dark screen with the white prompt waiting for you to type a command.

It was pretty boring to most people; however, it has evolved like the internet.

Most of its flavours today have a desktop version with an excellent screen, and pictures, as well visible folders.

In fact, Linux became one of the most stable operating systems even today.

Furthermore, as of today, every Android mobile device is based on Linux. Amazon Kindle devices are also based on Linux.

Now, if you ask me, I believe these devices are easy enough to handle and operate.

Well, Linux has changed, and the now, two decades later, everyone is aware of its existence, even if it's called something different. It has not stopped there of course. Cisco Systems are also based on Linux, and believe me; those are best, most stable, and fastest routers today exist.

Those babies are letting us use the internet with the speed that we have today.

However, if you might be more familiar with home based routers such as Linksys, ACER, LG, Motorola, Dell, Toshiba, Nokia, Sony, Sharp, Alcatel, Blackberry, Nexus, HTC, Google Glass, Archos, Samsung, Raspberry Pie, Pandora... well, they are all based on Linux operating system.

Besides cell phones and routers, there is other use of Android based systems too, such as in-car entertainment systems, Airplane entertainment systems, home theatre, gaming industry, digital security, and yet other devices, that are not even based on Earth.

Some other devices that are certainly notable, uses android based operating systems are used by NASA, such as Space Stations, Satellites, flight computes, even rockets.

Back to Bitcoin evolution, and think about where will it land in the next decade, or two?

I am not able to predict the future, however, if we might face a problem that required a solution, I am pretty sure that we will figure it out.

Bitcoin is getting it's fame already, it's only a matter of time to be world wide implemented, and to take over the world in some form.

Chapter 14 – Purchase Power

I often being asked this question: Keizer! Who should I ask for permission if I want to make a payment with Bitcoin?

So my answer is always the same: You do not need to ask anyone for any permission. You can buy and sell Bitcoin anytime you want. Day or night, in any country, all you need is an internet connection. Bitcoin is not regulated by any nation, as this is not a government currency.

You can buy Bitcoin, and become your bank, even if you are under aged. It is not like walking into a bank, and you must be at least 18 years old if you want to open an account. You can also buy Bitcoin even if you don't have a job.

When you go to the bank and asking for a bank account, they will ask you to bring proof from your workplace, stating your position, as well how many hours you work and how much is your wages. It is ridiculous, and no wonder why over 2 billion people have no bank account. Anyways, there is no permission required from anyone.

Getting paid in Bitcoin

In case you are a freelancer, and selling your services online, you might choose to get paid in Bitcoin. Again you don't need to ask for permission from anyone, and you can get paid in Bitcoin.

What can you buy?

Well, you can buy anything on the dark web—of course—I do not recommend that, as you might come across criminals who would try to steal or hack into your bitcoin wallet.

Some cyber criminals would even try to blackmail you. However, if you do not provide your details, you should be just fine.

Realistically, more services are excepting Bitcoin, such as Hotels, Restaurants, Coffee shops, even some takeaway shops are now offering payment method using Bitcoin.

Large retail companies are also accepting Bitcoin, such as Shopify, TigerDirect, and much more. To see how broad range it can be, you have to look around where you live. The big cities have all sort of offerings, such as:

- Theatre
- Taxi Service
- Bicycle rent
- Private Jets
- Pubs

Also, you may consider other large companies that are now accepting Bitcoin, such as:

- Dell
- Microsoft
- Zynga
- Reddit
- Wordpress.com
- Subway
- Expedia.com
- Virgin Galactic
- OK Cupid
- Stream
- Alza
- Lionsgate Films
- Badoo... And much more

By using Gift cards, multiple applications also allow customers to purchase on websites, such as:

- Amazon.com
- Walmart
- Target
- Nike
- GAP
- BEBE
- Sears
- Papa Johns
- Best Buy
- iTunes
- eBay
- Starbucks
- Zappos
- CVS Pharmacy
- The HOME depot... And much more.

I wanted you to know that some of the largest companies already adapting to the idea of accepting Bitcoin. Moreover, to understand the range of goods and services that can be purchased, please see the list of categories that you may choose from:

- Airline
- Automotive
- Beauty
- Clothing

- Department Stores
- e-Commerce
- Electronics
- Gas
- Gifts and Toys
- Grocery
- Health
- Home and Garden
- Home improvement
- Hotel
- Jewelry
- Movies
- Pets
- Restaurants
- Shoes
- Sporting goods

As you see, the categories of shopping options are keep on growing, and if you are more interested in what stores you can pay using Bitcoin, you might check what you have nearby you, or what online platforms can deliver to your area.

Chapter 15 – Get ready for the revolution

Why would I say that? – And what revolution? Well, you are reading this book; therefore you have an idea about Bitcoin; however, you can do a little test and see for yourself, where the rest of the world stands right now.

For example, I assume that you have some regular places that you often visit, even if not every day, but weekly or monthly. What you can do, is pick five or ten of them places where you typically purchase thinks like coffee, bread or milk, and when you just about to make your regular payment, ask the cashier if they accept Bitcoin.

I bet there are very few people out there, who would understand what you are on about. It is up to you, but you would be surprised how many people never even heard of Bitcoin or the word cryptocurrency.

I often ask shop owners if they accept Bitcoin, and see how they react, and I have to say most people are laughing, then say politely:, nooo, not yet." With a smiley face. I believe these are the individuals who have heard of Bitcoin previously; however, they have insufficient knowledge if there is any.

Most times people looking at me and ask me:,, What? What's that? NO!" meaning they have no clue, and not even interested what that is. In fact, they might think that I am from those funny, candid camera tv shows, so probably they just want me to pay and get out.

I respect the Blockchain technology behind Bitcoin, however I don't mean to pressure people to get into Bitcoin, especially to invest all your money; however, it is time to get familiar with it. In my next book, I will explain how to buy safely, as well how much should you invest as a beginner, and how to keep your Bitcoin safe against hackers.

Are we there yet?

I will be sincere here, and I tell you right now, that we are not there yet. Unfortunately not yet, in fact, we are looking at ten to fifteen years, but it might be two more decades.

I only wish if that's a lie, but I have to be realistic and understand where do we stand right now. First of all, the technology that we have is great, and we already have it all that required implementing Bitcoin everywhere; however, changes take time. There is an enormous amount of work needs to be done to get those changes completed.

The reality is that Blockchain start-ups don't need to implement changes; however, there are so many existing companies that are just so large to make all required changes in all their systems, and to do so, would probably take five to ten years.

People are not educated enough, Blockchain developers need years of studying, and to get ready to work, everyday learning is essential for the rest of their career.

It is true that currently, we haven't got enough man power to carry out such changes.

So, basically there is not enough engineers yet, not enough software developers yet, those who could setup, as well maintain the system.

And again, the worse is that people want to become millionaires by investing in technologies, like Bitcoin or Blockchain, but when it comes to studying it for years, than only few people to participate.

Marketplace

As I mentioned before, I guarantee you that those ten people you are going to ask about Bitcoin will have no clue, even they might have heard about it, they are probably don't have any, don't know how to buy or how to get paid in Bitcoin.

What it tells you is the market simply not ready for the change. Some places don't even accept credit cards yet.

Credit cards are not a new invention, yet many places still don't take it as a paying method. Some other places do accept it, but you have to spend at least five, some other places at least ten dollars, otherwise have to pay with cash.

Nation states

If Bitcoin would be implemented everywhere in the world, there would be no more US dollar or Canadian Dollar, neither Japanese yen, therefore once all those would disappear, everyone would have to start thinking differently. Are we ready for that yet? I don't think so, but it's only my opinion.

It will take some time to adapt, but eventually will happen.

Get involved

Finally, I would like to close this chapter with good news; actually, it's excellent news! If you are getting familiar now with Bitcoin, there is no better time for sure! Faster you get involved and learn about the future of money, more comfortable your future will be. This is a fact.

Same thing, as everyone has to find out how to open a bank account at some point, in the future, everyone has to learn how to open a Bitcoin account, and to be honest, opening a Bitcoin account way easier than opening a bank account! Blockchain does not care if you are under age, neither your sex, or occupation.

Blockchain will not ask your wages, or for proof of address, it does not care your race, neither how you look like, in fact, it does not care if you are a human or not. Yes, that's right, in the future, machines can have a Bitcoin account on the Blockchain. Furthermore, they will be able to communicate with each other, and make transactions that you do today. For example, your fridge will know exactly when it will run out of Orange Juice, and it will be able to order it from Amazon, than an Amazon drone will be able to deliver your orange juice in no time! Once again, get involved in the future of money, talk to people who already involved, read books, and educate yourself. Understand how Blockchain works, and see how powerful it is, so that will give you more confidence for better understanding.

In case you are not interested in M2M aka machine to machine learning, that's fine, however, there are other reasons too, to get involved. If you look at Chapter 1 in this book, you might realize that on the 4th of August 2017, the value of Bitcoin was $2891,79; however just last night Bitcoin has reached the 4000 dollar mark, in fact it has hit all time highest mark of 4208.39 dollars.

#	Name	Symbol	Market Cap	Price	Circulating Supply	Volume (24h)	% 1h	% 24h
1	Bitcoin	BTC	$66,752,546,384	$4044.46	16,504,687	$3,212,950,000	1.42%	5.41%
2	Ethereum	ETH	$28,147,402,494	$299.53	93,970,956	$1,396,240,000	3.12%	-5.09%
3	Ripple	XRP	$6,486,083,784	$0.169117	38,352,642,160 *	$117,671,000	1.27%	-4.11%
4	Bitcoin Cash	BCH	$5,192,978,882	$314.92	16,489,886	$125,378,000	3.40%	-2.64%
5	Litecoin	LTC	$2,422,477,517	$46.19	52,443,432	$280,819,000	0.75%	2.37%
6	NEM	XEM	$2,400,021,000	$0.266669	8,999,999,999 *	$8,992,120	0.85%	-6.95%
7	NEO	NEO	$2,331,185,000	$46.62	50,000,000 *	$290,322,000	10.29%	37.17%
8	IOTA	MIOTA	$2,064,587,842	$0.742783	2,779,530,283 *	$36,012,100	1.67%	8.51%
9	Dash	DASH	$1,528,440,947	$204.08	7,489,567	$39,390,200	-0.32%	-2.10%

These details are from coinmarketcap.com for your reference. Mainly in the last nine days, we have experienced around 40% growth. Meaning, if you have invested in Bitcoin, an amount pf 500 dollars two weeks ago, today that would worth around 700 dollars.

Now if you are a trader and you would invest $50K, within two weeks you could have made over $20K without even to be obligated to pay tax on it. There are millions, if not billions of people who don't make $20 even within a year, that's alone, should be just enough proof what a single cryptocurrency can do, more specifically Bitcoin. I am sure that you recognize the muscle of Bitcoin now, as well what path is going to, and indeed, hope that you have begun to like this young, yet super influential cryptocurrency!

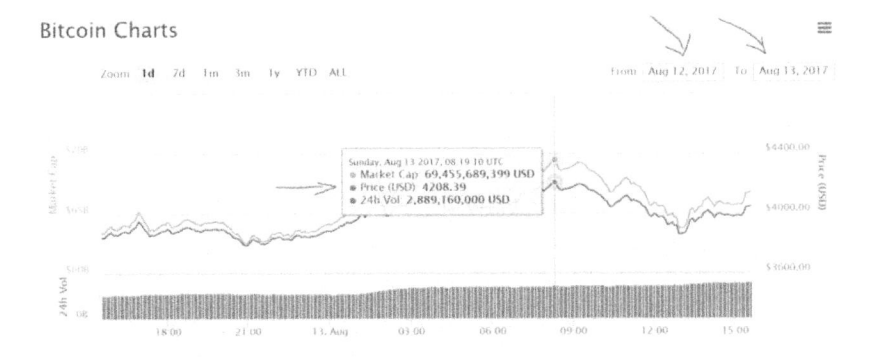

Bonus Chapter – How to get paid in Bitcoin

Would you like to get paid in Cryptocurrency from your employer?

Never better to start than now! There is a company called Bitwage, that are now able to help you to get paid in Bitcoin, directly from the company that you are working for.

Bitwage is an international wage payment and staffing solution, that built on top of the Bitcoin Blockchain.

Payments:

Paying a domestic employee is straightforward. All you need is an account number, and you can start paying an employee. However, when start making international payments, that's when it becomes a little complicated. Unfortunately, many banks don't allow international payments to be made online. Instead, you have to confirm your payment over the phone, or worse in person.

When the workers are receiving the money they have worked for; they have to deal with unfavourable exchange rates, due to the money have been moved through international systems. As a result, we can see and experience, that freelancers are changing is higher, or even rejecting clients that are international, just because of these issues.

Imagine there are two different banks, that one resides in Bangladesh and the other in the United states. Each of them has their ledger system to keep their records up to date. However, there are some issues between the banks once they begin to interact. Because these banks have private ledgers, they have to work out between themself how they are going to send 1000 dollars from one to another. Back in the 1800-s, they had to put gold on the boot and ship it through the Atlantic Ocean; however, we are lot more efficient than that.

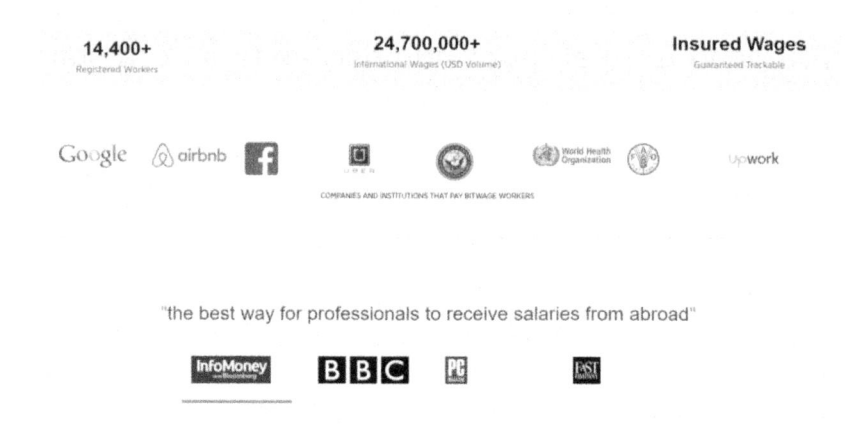

14,400+	24,700,000+	Insured Wages
Registered Workers	International Wages (USD Volume)	Guaranteed Trackable

Google airbnb f 　 　 World Health Organization upwork

COMPANIES AND INSTITUTIONS THAT PAY BITWAGE WORKERS

"the best way for professionals to receive salaries from abroad"

InfoMoney BBC PC FAST

We have the internet, and many people believe that the current banking system is allowing easily to proceed with the international payment transfers; however, it is not true. Because both banks have a private ledger system, there is an issue of trust. To bridge these trust issues, the corresponding banking system was created.

Banks have build relationships with other banks they trust, by doing so, they have to develop corresponding accounts to each other. Because of different rules in different countries, they have built a chain of banks. So what is happening is that in Bangladesh a small bank first moves money to a big bank in Bangladesh, then to another large bank to the US. Then this large bank in the US will transfer to the small bank to it's original destination. However, if there is a currency conversion in the process, there will be even more intermediaries involved.

With each intermediary, there is a cost and delay, that is around 3-5 days on average, as well a cost on a currency exchange that is an average of 8%.

All these efficiencies have to do with the fact that there is a lack of trust in a private ledger system. However, with Bitcoin, thinks are indeed completely different.

From a high level, the Blockchain is a public ledger, that can maintain high level of privacy. So using this system, an e-mail can confirm the transaction, by having a link in the e-mail.

That link, is access to a highly secured public ledger, that undeniably proves that the money was sent from the small bank in Bangladesh to another small bank to the US.

Therefore, we no longer need any of those intermediaries, who approves the process, as well delaying the transactions and taking a fee.

As a result, international payments and Bitcoin are together, making payments across borders ever closer to the speed and ease to the domestic payment.

While this is happening, foreign remote workers or companies can maintain relationships a lot easier than before.

Reputation of an employee or employer

Employees know they must have an attractive profile, which provides good reputation to get quality work.

However, reputation can be easily manipulated by hacking profiles or faking CV-s. Using the Blockchain, you can achieve a reputation system that can not be faked.

As it turns out, how much you get paid, for how long and by who, are all objective statistics that are good for your reputation in an object of manner.

For example, if you are an HR recruiter, working for a company for year in full time, then another year for part time, that's value. Or if you are a network engineer who has been having a raise in every year in the past for years, that's another value.

All these information is valuable reputation. What turns out is that all these information is recorded on a Bitcoin transaction.

Therefore by receiving wages through a Bitcoin mechanism, you can have forever your reputation recorded on the Blockchain, in a decentralized way, from any client who pays you.

bitWAGE

bitwage.com

This is already happening, and remote workers are already receiving wages to obtain a Blockchain reputation. Unlike a subjective system that ends up producing lower quality workers, however they introduce themselves as high quality, using this payment status, it is indeed tough to manipulate the reputation mechanism.

This will help companies as well to trust in the reputation mechanism, and as a result, you will get a very efficient market between remote workers and enterprises. Bitcoin and Blockchain have been bridging these efficiencies and continued to do so.

In the future, companies will be made of decentralized work forces, which are glued together. Corporations and workers alike, will be able to find the perfect fit with one another, through objective payment reputation, with no differentiation between international and domestic payments.

Local workers will be empowered all over the world, while companies can leverage the competitive advantages of a diverse global workforce. Workers will be able to receive their wages faster and cheaper, while those payments can act as a reputation mechanism to help them find their next job.

If you like the idea of the future of payroll, either as an employee or as an employer, you might want to take a look at bitwages.com and find out more.

Conclusion

Thank you for purchasing this book. I hope this title has provided some insights into what is really behind the curtains when it comes to the future of money.

I have tried to favour every reader by avoiding technical terms on how Bitcoin works that currently flooding the market worldwide.

However, as I mentioned few times, to fully understand how Bitcoin works, you may choose to read my books on Blockchain:

Volume 1 – Blockchain – Beginners Guide
Volume 2 – Blockchain – Advanced Guide

Volume 2 is very technical, however, tried my best to use everyday English, and making sure that everyone can understand each of the technologies and their importance, and how they are combined.

My upcoming book on Bitcoin will provide more details on how to invest safely, and what kind of wallets you required before purchasing any Cryptocurrency.

I will also provide guidance, on how you can become a miner by renting equipment, as well how you can start mining digital money using your laptop, or even your Android phone.

Lastly, if you enjoyed the book, please take some time to share your thoughts and post a review. It would be highly appreciated!

BITCOIN
Invest in Digital Gold

Volume 2

by
Keizer Söze

Copyright
All rights reserved. No part of this book may be reproduced in any form or by any electronic, print or mechanical means, including information storage and retrieval systems, without permission in writing from the publisher.

Copyright © 2017 Keizer Söze

Disclaimer

This Book is produced with the goal of providing information that is as accurate and reliable as possible. Regardless, purchasing this Book can be seen as consent to the fact that both the publisher and the author of this book are in no way experts on the topics discussed within and that any recommendations or suggestions that are made herein are for entertainment purposes only.

Professionals should be consulted as needed before undertaking any of the action endorsed herein.
Under no circumstances will any legal responsibility or blame be held against the publisher for any reparation, damages, or monetary loss due to the information herein, either directly or indirectly.

This declaration is deemed fair and valid by both the American Bar Association and the Committee of Publishers Association and is legally binding throughout the United States.

The information in the following pages is broadly considered to be a truthful and accurate account of facts and as such any inattention, use or misuse of the information in question by the reader will render any resulting actions solely under their purview. There are no scenarios in which the publisher or the original author of this work can be in any fashion deemed liable for any hardship or damages that may befall the reader or anyone else after undertaking information described herein.

Additionally, the information in the following pages is intended only for informational purposes and should thus be thought of as universal. As befitting its nature, it is presented without assurance regarding its prolonged validity or interim quality. Trademarks that are mentioned are done without written consent and can in no way be considered an endorsement from the trademark holder.

Introduction

Congratulations on purchasing this book and thank you for doing so.

This book is an excellent beginner's guide to understanding what Bitcoin has to offer, and how it changes the future of doing business. The contents avoid technical details to provide a better understanding to those, who are new to this technology. There are certain terms that some technical background in Information Technology would help. However, it's not necessary. Everyday English has been used through this book to avoid confusion.

This book will take you by the hand, and show you step-by-step, how digital currency was born by analyzing historical data. For better understanding, first, this books is beginning with a brief introduction of why to consider Bitcoin at the first place, and why often called as Digital Gold. Furthermore, it takes a look at why is much likely, that the value of Bitcoin will hit 1 million dollars.

Next, we take a look at some examples and understand why Bitcoin is at its early days, and why it's not late to start investing. Following by wallet technology overview, explaining the key differences between hot wallets, cold wallets, and how to find out what suits you best. Next, I will recommend the best hot wallets, as well the best cold wallets that exist on the market, following by providing you all details on where and how to purchase them.

The book will carry on explaining Bitcoin ATMs, their purpose, how to locate them, as well how to use them for both: buying and selling Bitcoin anytime, securely, and offline.

Next, I will introduce the best online cryptocurrency trading platforms, and explain the key differences, as well their pros & cons. Next, will enclose how to recognize online scammers, and teach you how not to be fooled by online thieves. Finally, I will explain why it's profitable to trade with Bitcoin, and explain how to become a mixture of both investor and trader.

In the Bonus Chapter, I will provide some basics of Bitcoin mining, and its history, then finishing off on how you can mine Bitcoin using your old laptop, or even your Android phone with a free online software.

There are plenty of books on this subject in the market, thanks again for choosing this one! Every effort was made to ensure the book is riddled with as much useful information as possible. Please enjoy!

Chapter 1 - Why consider Bitcoin

For the first time in human existence, we have a secondary option to a none governmental controlled currency. This is awesome! This is when you and I, in fact, anyone can participate. This, itself is why the most important, however, let me expand on it with further detail.

There are many cryptocurrencies out there; however Bitcoin was the first amongst them. Cryptocurrency works, and it's simply put, provides additional options. There are multiple opportunities time to time that could potentially benefit you and your family. However Bitcoin is one of the best options, and I will tell you exactly why. If you look at the current banking system and understand how they manipulate the inflation rates and lending out money that hard working people saved over the years, you know that is absolutely ridiculous.

For example, I am saving 1000 dollars over the years, that I will give to the bank, so they can give me 1% interests after a year. Of course not allowed to touch it. However, if I want to use it, not only all my interests would be lost, but I would be even charged for it.

So, then I choose to keep that money in the bank, then you would go to the bank and borrow that money, however, once you would do that, your interest rate to pay it back would be 20%, or even more.

Now, this is over the limit. Don't get me wrong, and I do understand banks have bills to pay too, as well hard working employees, security, computers, antiviruses, firewalls, and all; however, the option remains.

In 2008 when there was a largest financial breakdown in history, banks have decided to provide money, as a bailout for insurance companies, car companies. They have began printing paper money like crazy, causing devaluation of all those existing hard working earned money. Therefore it has devalued the economy too, and increasingly created inflation. Once the interest rate is getting higher, you have to think about surviving.

In case you have lot's of money in the bank, and tomorrow we are going to hit the next financial breakdown, the banks can decide to not giving you any money. In fact, they can call in bankruptcy, meaning, you will never see your money again.

It has happened over the last 50 years in multiple countries, and people, as well small businesses have become poor, or worse, homeless. Financial crisis will happen again, and it will happen more often than before. Firstly, because the last one back in 2008 has not dealt with, all have happened is a workaround, but no real fix.

Secondly, the world debt has only grown since, and soon will be time for demanding those debts. The problem will be the same as last time or the time before.

The debt will not be paid by the banks, who are responsible for creating the debt in the first place, but the bank will demand from those who have mortgages or other interests to pay back to the banks.

To think otherwise would be certainly unwise. The money that banks have, well is a bit of funny money; indeed it's kind a believable money.

Those times long gone when gold or silver was backing money up, those were real money, however, nowadays it's only numbers, or digits, that the banks told us that is worth something. Meaning worth nothing.

What Bitcoin provides us is a revolutionary currency that not controlled by the government, neither any bank or the Federal reserve system, therefore providing us an additional option to FIAT money. You can buy Bitcoin using multiple different mobile phone based application for free.

You can also use the desktop version of applications, or even individual exchanges, or even from local Bitcoin meet ups. Additionally, nearly any currency is exchangeable to Bitcoin. Therefore there is no excuse.

Another thing is that Bitcoin is not just some sort Day trading option, something that you can invest only. However, you can also earn Bitcoin. I have explained in my previous book:

Bitcoin Blueprint - Volume 1

You can receive Bitcoin, using the company called Bitwage, while it doesn't matter what company you are working for. Besides to Bitwage, there are other freelancing companies too, where you can provide your services in exchange for Bitcoin.

Some of those online freelancing platforms are Upwork, FIVERR; however there are much more out there, and with a simple google search you find much more. So once you have Bitcoin, you can make a transaction to any destination in the world.

Imagine that you want to send only 100 dollars to China, and you have to deal with high bank changes, as well currency exchange charges, not to mention the minimum five days delays.

Of course you might use PayPal or other trusted third party services; however the transfer delay could take even longer, and the fees are also will become higher, which are at least 5%.

In the other hand, transferring Bitcoin, the transfer charges are on average of 0.5% to 1%, independent of how much value of Bitcoin you are about to transfer, additionally the transfer will be immediate, and in a maximum of 10 minutes, it will be validated on the blockchain forever. As you can see, when using Bitcoin or any other cryptocurrency,

YOU ARE THE BANK.

You have to understand that are no other intermediaries required for you to make a transfer to anywhere in the world.

The only thing is needed really is to have a Bitcoin account for the person that you are to transfer to. Bitcoin account can be downloaded to a cell phone in less than 2 minutes. There is a misconception where people believe that once you lose your phone, your Bitcoin will be lost too. This is not true.

You can back up your phone, and even you would lose your phone or break it, using another device you can log in to your Bitcoin account anytime, from anywhere in the world and access your account.

As soon as you recall your account on the new device, you will be able to make additional transfers or exchanges to different Fiat currencies, or even cryptocurrencies, all you need is internet access.

As I mentioned before, finally we have access to purchase Bitcoin, or any other cryptocurrency using our phone, and this is from our own will, instead of asking for appointments from the bank to open bank accounts, and all those annoying procedures.

Additionally, it has been observed that each time when a nation's fiat currency devalues, Bitcoin price increases.

This is easily explained by those who affected, learned that hard working earned money can be lost because of government manipulations, and it's time to put savings into Bitcoin.

The worse of all is that more than 2 billion people around the world have no bank account, and those people might be not allowed to have an account due to the banks; however, some others may just don't want to participate as a bank account holder.

We all can have a Bitcoin account, and all we need is a phone, or even if we can not afford a phone, all we need is internet access when we wish to make a transfer.

This is opening another new market, as those who were afraid of local government or local mafia, they can simply have all their money in Bitcoin, registered on the blockchain.

Other noted accomplishments, such as charities that are also corrupted, now can freely receive the exact amount of money that you or I would intend them to receive.

It is very similar to crowdfunding, and the concepts are simple. If I want to give 100 dollars to a charity, how come they are only receiving 30% of the sums of money?

Well, the rest of the money goes to the currency exchanges, banks fees, marketing specialists, and whatever people who are part of the setup in the first place.

Instead, I can transfer the exact amount of money as person to person, or person to business manner, and I will know exactly how much they will receive as the transaction will be recorded on the blockchain.

Furthermore, speed of implementation. Imagine that someone requires 1000 dollars as soon as possible, and you choose a bank for transferring.

Imagine that the money only will reach the destination, and become withdrawable in the next five days.

That's crazy slow, especially in 2017, is just utterly ridiculous!

Imagine that five days later the money would be too late because someone would require something urgently, the good will wouldn't be enough if you choose the bank.

Then again, in the other hand using Bitcoin, the transfer is immediate and gets validated within a maximum of ten minutes from the time of transfer.

Not enough reason to consider Bitcoin? Then let's dive in!

Chapter 2 – Peer-to-Peer Economy

Yes, you have heard of Bitcoin, as well Ethereum, Monero, Litecoin, and they are indeed are cryptocurrencies. What you have to understand, is they are all functioning on the blockchain. Without the blockchain platform, they would not exist.

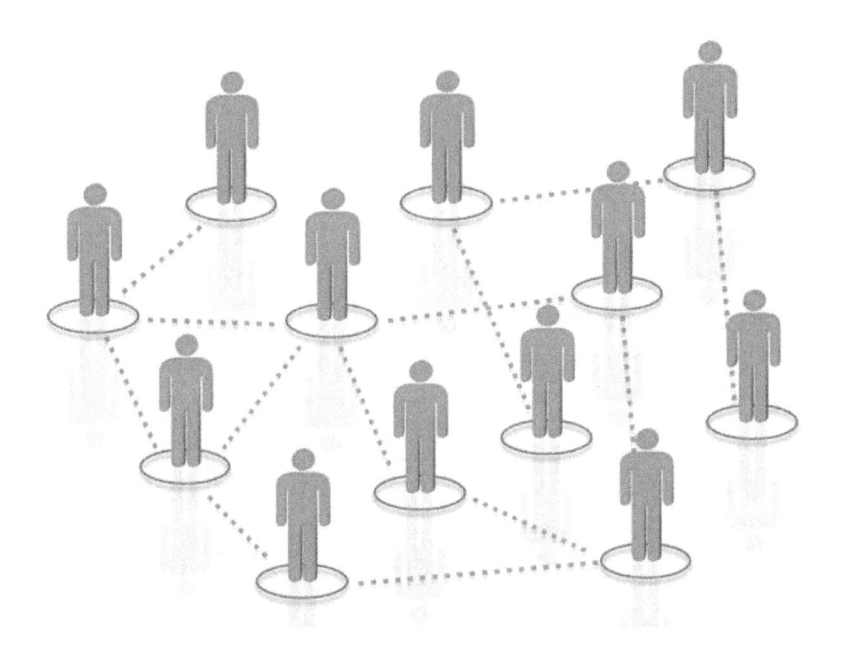

Therefore, firstly you have to understand what Satoshi Nakamoto has done with Bitcoin. He was able to solve the problem of manipulating code. Before his invention, nothing was stopping you to copying the same digits and sending to multiple destinations. Having created the blockchain, Satoshi was able to solve the problem. This, has now changed the world of posting digital code, so let's look at an example.

If I were to send you 100 dollars worth of Bitcoin from my account, I would have 100 dollars less of my code. Then you would send that code to your friend, you wouldn't have it anymore, as your friend would have it, and so on...

However before the blockchain, it was impossible, in fact, people have been working on this since the late 70's, yet no one was able to solve this issue. Against the centralized banking system, Bitcoin transactions are now empowering the end-users by becoming the bank itself.

So basically there is no inflation that the banks or governments can manipulate, neither controlled currency of what I can or I can not use, and most certainly no interests rates. With Bitcoin, there is no quantitative easing, simply because it has a pre set algorithm that set's it to 21 million Bitcoins.

There will be only 21 million Bitcoin mined ever. Therefore you can't print more Bitcoin, neither can control the inflation, nor the interests rate. Bitcoin is a real decentralized peer-to-peer system that can store v

alue. Those, who unbanked, now may become their bank, and more people using Bitcoin all over the world, and more network effect will be; therefore those people can create an even better peer-to-peer economy.

Freedom of choice

What freedom of choice does, is that you can send Bitcoin all over the world by using your account, instead of your name. Even though your address will be registered on the blockchain once the transaction is validated, it's done, however, your name will not be there.

When you think about it, anonymously sending money from anywhere to anywhere, to anyone, at any time, it is power. The reality is the majority of the world is living in a particular government society, and they do not have the same freedom as others.

Therefore it is complicated for them to speak up, and this is why you can see a huge rise of Bitcoin in countries such as India, where there is a currency war right now. As you see, some of those people can not speak up, they are fed up with the government, as well their money track down system, and now they have a choice to opt out into a Cryptocurrency such as Bitcoin.

Opt out to currency, that is own by a peer-to-peer network, where they can take control of their hard worked earned money.

Again, what Bitcoin-Blockchain system does, is designed in a certain way, where it doesn't matter where you live, or what race you have, even what is your religion or political view, simply because anyone can join the global peer-to-peer system.

Bitcoin creates a digital identity, instead of providing your name, in a decentralized manner.

Chapter 3 - Is Bitcoin dead?

Short answer: yes. Bitcoin is dead, in fact, Bitcoin is so dead that poor Bitcoin has died 151 times already! ...yet it still exists!
If you are thinking how is that even possible, then let me elaborate on this topic with further details.

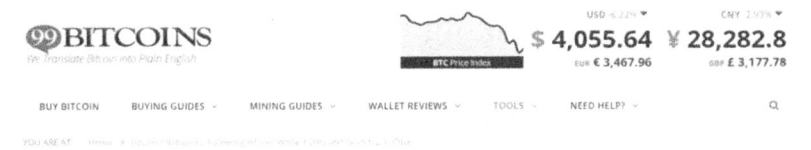

Bitcoin Obituaries
Bitcoin has died 151 times

Most times when Bitcoin makes it to the news, often have some negativity. Bitcoin is most famous of being a criminal currency and thinks like that. Well, Bitcoin can be transferred all over the world with anonymity; therefore criminals love to use it.

Should we burn it to the ground then? We should right?
The reality is that criminals use cars too. Should we burn the cars as well?

Oh no, we can't, because someone would lose out on profit. How about cell phones? What I understand, is that criminals use cell phones too! We must stop producing mobile phones too. But you know what? I heard that criminals using the internet, and Facebook too! So we have no choice, but to kill the internet and facebook and twitter, (especially twitter). Common now!

Or, is it just about the currency? Then again, criminals do use hard cash, as well have bank accounts and making transfers too, some of them also paying tax, and bills, but anyway... Like everything else in the world, can be used for good as well for bad intensions.

Computers can be utilized for studying as well hacking. Police officers have guns, and criminals have guns too. Michelin chefs have very sharp knives, and some underground thugs have even sharper knives too.

We can't just stop producing everything in the world! Wake up! Not you, but those who apparently believe that Bitcoin is only for criminal use. This is ridiculous, however many people still think that Bitcoin is a money of the criminals like rapists, drug dealers, arms dealers, terrorists and all the evil that exists.

I am not saying they don't use it, yes they certainly do, but Bitcoin can change the life of billions, and that will be appreciated and should be focused on. Criminals will be criminals anyway, but please stop spreading nonsense about something that is a truly revolutionary technology. Unfortunately, Bitcoin has been introduced with a bad reputation, and this has triggered to create even more fake news over the years.

Another one is when Bitcoin hits a milestone in value. Bitcoin was dead when it has reached $100, then died again when it hit $200, then again when it hit $1000, and so on and so forth... However the value of one Bitcoin today is $4137.33. Today is 18th of August 2017.

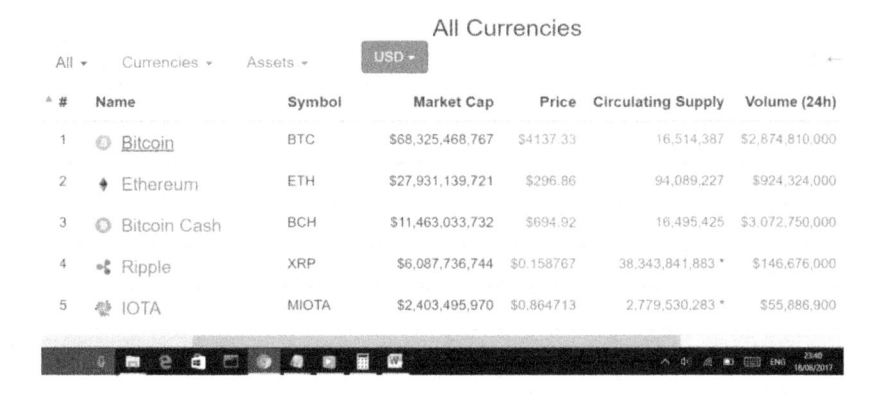

#	Name	Symbol	Market Cap	Price	Circulating Supply	Volume (24h)
1	Bitcoin	BTC	$68,325,468,767	$4137.33	16,514,387	$2,874,810,000
2	Ethereum	ETH	$27,931,139,721	$296.86	94,089,227	$924,324,000
3	Bitcoin Cash	BCH	$11,463,033,732	$694.92	16,495,825	$3,072,750,000
4	Ripple	XRP	$6,087,736,744	$0.158767	38,343,841,883 *	$146,676,000
5	IOTA	MIOTA	$2,403,495,970	$0.864713	2,779,530,283 *	$55,886,900

There is a website that is specializing in; Bitcoin is Dead."

This site is a collection of all those news where Bitcoin was in the news as a dead currency for all sort of reasons. If you can click on the following link, it will take you right there:

https://99bitcoins.com/bitcoinobituaries/

First time when Bitcoin was dead, it was in December 2010. Since that painful event, Bitcoin has died another 150 times, yet still, exist. So what we can learn from it, is more and more Bitcoin will die, more it will hit the news. Therefore more people will hear those fake news when Bitcoin has died.

When you think about it, imagine that you heard in 2010 that Bitcoin is dead, then you read another article in 2011 where Bitcoin is dead again, but then in 2012 you will hear it in the telly that Bitcoin is dead, in fact, Bitcoin has died in 2013, 17 times. So, obviously something isn't right. Anyways, I wanted to share with you this link and another fake news: Bitcoin is dead! This time dead really, because in 2017 until middle of August it has died 32 times already.

Ok, maybe you not going to believe me, so I will tell you the truth instead: Bitcoin will carry on end up dead again and again in the news.
However,

...Bitcoin is here to stay!

Chapter 4 - Will Bitcoin hit $1million?

Now, this is a more interesting question, and again the short answer is: yes. Yes, Bitcoin will hit the value of 1 million dollars for sure; however, the real question should sound like this: When will Bitcoin hit a $1million mark?

As you see the real question is the date, instead of: does Bitcoin has a capability or not.

There is a huge industry around Bitcoin, and people already made a fortune of investing into it.

Due to Bitcoin's value increasing over the years from cents to dollars, then from hundreds of dollars to thousand dollars, and only this year from one thousand to two thousand, then all the way up to 4500 dollars, it is possible to see Bitcoin reach 1 Million dollars.

There are analysis, where predictions of Bitcoin can capture between one and ten percent of the global forex market. That implies that the price of Bitcoin could rise between 100,000 to a million dollars.

Most of the people who on the sidelines and not buying Bitcoin today will start to buy Bitcoin when it reaches 5000 dollars. The greater percentage of the people will invest into Bitcoin when it starts to get over ten thousand.

Some predictions already stated that Bitcoin value would reach 10000 dollars by 2010.

There will be ups and down like any other technology, however as I mentioned earlier, Bitcoin is here to stay, and some other notable people like the CEO of Zappos has been predicted that Bitcoin can reach the value of between 500,000 to a million dollars by the year of 2025.

Most people only see the charts, and thinking how high it can go, however, if you begin to count backward instead of looking at the charts, you may look at it in another way, which is this:

This is a transactional currency, and It is a store of value. A such, like it, is a product and a service competing on a very substantial market for storing value and transactional currency.

Therefore, you should look at the size of market of that, as well how big the market share, then you can start calculating what Bitcoin can realistically take in a realistic timeframe.

Once you ask that question, then you will come up with the market capitalization of Bitcoin total.

Next, you divide that, by the number of Bitcoin in circulation by the estimated time, then you can come up with some between two million to five million dollars per Bitcoin.

My suggestion is this: if you buy at least one Bitcoin as soon as possible, that could be just enough for you to become a millionaire in the future.

Bitcoin is a currency of the future, no doubt of that, however you have to look at it on a bigger scale and understand that Bitcoin itself would be worthless, however, because it's scaling on the blockchain technology, it will become not only a currency, but a payment system.

This is because of the blockchain encryption, that has a greater ability to bring more of the world of the population out of poverty than anything else we have ever experienced.

It is truly one of the most important inventions of the history of human kind, and certainly most important invention since the internet.

This is going to improve the lives of every single person on the planet.

If Bitcoin will become a real money and excepted worldwide in the next ten years, it can become easily worth of 1 million dollars.

If you look at the value of US dollars in circulation, that might be between 5-15 trillion dollars, then divide it by the total amount of Bitcoin in circulation that is currently 16 million.

Next, if you use even the higher value of dollars calculated, that is 15 trillion, next let's calculate how many Bitcoin will be in circulation within ten years, and that is around 18 million, all is needed is to divide that figure, and it comes out to 833,333 dollars.

Well not exactly 1 million dollars, but it is a very close digit. Of course, Bitcoin might become only mainstream within 20 years.

However, due to our current technology and having the internet, we have learned, that this process can become quicker.

In fact, there are researches shows, to accomplish something that is related to technology as well global payment systems using the internet, we can speed up the process in average of 3 times faster.

If that figure is accurate, that could also mean that Bitcoin can be accepted worldwide within seven years.

If you would calculate the seven years, instead of the ten, using the same formula as I have just exhibited earlier, it could mean that Bitcoin can even expand beyond 1 million per coin.

Chapter 5 – Are you late for Bitcoin?

Should you invest in Bitcoin?

First of all, if you are asking yourself a question, it might be a wrong question to begin with. The question you should ask is:, when will you invest in Bitcoin" However let elaborate on this topic.

The time will come where financial systems will collapse, or people will lose faith in their government, or worse, when the inflation makes you homeless.

Those times will be when Bitcoin should be looked at, as a vehicle to invest in it. However, you may choose to see Bitcoin not as an investment, but a new opportunity. If you start to think differently, it might become more apparent to you, that is not just can become the best investment you would ever do, but merely a new opportunity to try out something that you have never experienced before.

You might aim to become a Bitcoin millionaire; however, you don't have to, at least not at first. Instead understand first what Bitcoin can provide to you, as well to everyone on this planet. If you look at those who already become a Bitcoin millionaire, you might realize that there is a pattern between them.

That model comes down to faith in Bitcoin, as well a full awareness of what exactly Bitcoin is. So first of all, you might be overwhelmed like one of my friend Baggio, who want to invest 1000 Euro, but he hasn't even got a wallet yet, in fact, he has no clue what the wallet is in the first place.

There are people, who have saved of 10-20K or even more and bought Bitcoin with it, then some of them find themselves unable to access their wallet, hence all money lost in the cloud.

Instead, buy today for 50 dollars, but at first definitely no more than 100 dollars worth of Bitcoin, and start to understand how it works.

Make a payment first, you might buy something on Fiverr, or Upwork, or even purchase something on Overstock.com or some of the Shopify stores, either way, my point is, to make a payment with Bitcoin.

Then you might try out some of the exchanges and see what best works out for you, and what platform you prefer. My point here is this: do not think that you become rich overnight, or think of it as a fast instant cash, and it is because Bitcoin doesn't work like that.

As I mentioned a few times already, Bitcoin is here to stay. Therefore you have to look at it in the long term, as it will influence our lives in the future.

Again, the point is not how much it will worth and when, instead, take this opportunity, by start putting your toe in the water, and begin to understand the system that we are entering. It will transform everything that is currently part of our life, therefore it is a good idea to have some basic knowledge, as a minimum.

Society is changing rapidly, especially with the technology that we are using today, and if you want to be ahead of the game, and want to understand where the human society is heading, such as automation or machine learning using Blockchain, it is certainly mind-blowing what the future will bring us. A future that is already in the testing environment, and the stable root, Blockchain already in place. Those that are not interested right now, it's ok, however those people will not read this book anyways.

Those that are not interested today, one day, that will come soon by the way, will realize that it might have been better to get involved a bit earlier. However, if you have no clue what Bitcoin is or where it's heading, and this is your first book on Bitcoin, and you already made it to this chapter, then you already involved!

When it comes to a second option of transferring money on a medium, most people think and might choose another bank, Paypal or Payoneer, but you have another option. Or at last you are aware of it, and that itself can help out many people.

Bitcoin has been helping out millions of people already in the last few years, and it's only warming up. Of course, at the same time, getting stronger in value, as well in good reputation, and getting more accepted in many other countries too.

Chapter 6 – 11 Reasons to invest in Bitcoin

I have explained many reasons why you should invest in Bitcoin; however this time I will try to summarize them for you to have a better reference guide when it comes to this question:

**What are the possible reasons that you should invest in Bitcoin?
Here it comes, so get ready!**

1. Solves multiple issues: You don't need a bank, anyone can have a wallet, and it's free. You can send money to any person in the world at any time, with a little fee.

2. People in under developed countries, can have access to Bitcoin, and all it's required is Internet access

3. No central governance, therefore no one can control your money.

4. Optional: Nobody forces you to have Bitcoin. All through most countries, you must have your home currency when you go shopping; however, you can have Bitcoin too, in any country that you live in.

5. No single point of failure due to its peer-to-peer network

6. No Inflation, basically there is no continuous injection of Bitcoin into the marketplace, due to its fixed supply to 21 million.

7. Growing demand: while there is a rise in demand, the value per Bitcoin will continuously increase

8. Legalization of Bitcoin: there are more and more countries where Bitcoin already legalized such as US, UK, Australia, New Zealand, Netherland, Ireland, France, Belgium, Spain, Portugal, Malta, Greece, Bulgaria, Italy, Sweden, Russia, Norway, Iceland, Finland, Lithuania, Denmark, Estonia, Slovenia, Slovakia, Romania, Poland, Germany, Croatia, Czech Republic, Vietnam, Singapur, Thailand, Malaysia, Indonesia, Philippines, Taiwan, South Korea, Japan, Hong Kong, China, Pakistan, India, Lebanon, Jordan, Israel, Cyprus, Columbia, Chile, Brazil, Argentina, Nicaragua, Canada, Zimbabwe, South Africa, Nigeria.

NOTE: This data is according to the date of August, 2017.

9. Decentralized ledger system: Bitcoin is running on the technology called Blockchain,

that has become very famous in recent years for its security; therefore the system is fully trusted. Bitcoin was the first application of the blockchain technology.

10. Respected by influenced people: Bill Gates has stated that Bitcoin is better than the single currency, however amongst others, such as Richard Branson, or Warren Buffett, John McAfee, and much more. In fact, John believes so much in Bitcoin that he has predicted that by 2020 a value of Bitcoin will reach 500,000 dollars. Besides all the famous names, there are prominent companies as well who accept Bitcoin as a payment method on their platforms such as Microsoft, Expedia, Dell, Subway, Reddit, Steam, Alza, Virgin Galactic, and much more.

11. Early adopters. There is a graph called S curve that defines the adoption of technology by humans. This chart exhibits the types of people who and when they get involved in a particular technology in a percentage.

S curve has been studied before on an adoption of multiple technologies over the years, for such as Telephone, Electricity, Auto, Radio, Refrigerator, Stove, Washing machine, Dishwasher, Microwave, Colour TV, Air Conditioner, Computer, and Cell Phone

The S curve tells us, that in any community, there are five different types of people or adopter groups. These groups can be categorized by the time it takes them to adapt to a given innovation or new behavior. To identify what groups already approved the change and which groups have adopted to the innovation in different points in time. I describe them in order, so please find the adopter groups as below:

- Innovators > 2.5%
- Early Adopters > 13.5%
- Early majority > 34%
- Late majority > 34%
- Laggards > 16%

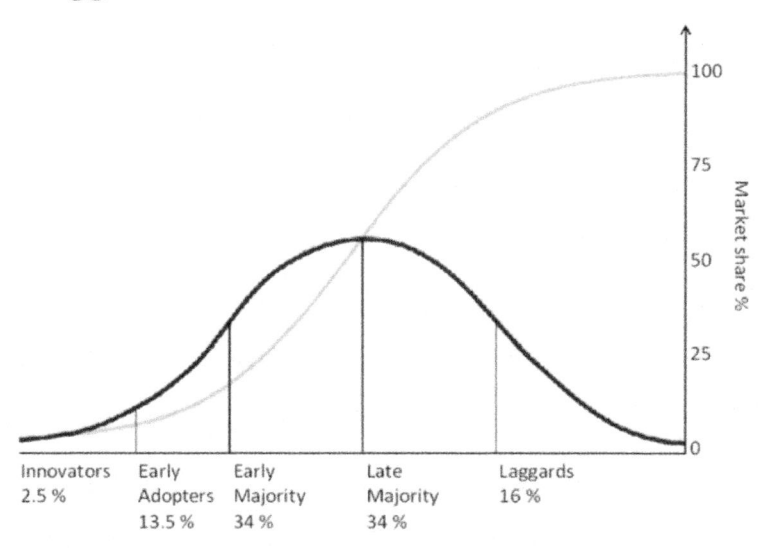

Now that's being said, Bitcoin exists since 8.5 years, and all 21million Bitcoin will be thoroughly mined by 2140.

Meaning the actual mining process will take around 131 years to fully complete, calculated since 2009.

That means, we are probably not Innovators anymore, however as of 2017, eight years on the run, and we have another 123 years left until all Bitcoin will be in circulation, I believe that we are in the age of Early Adopters.

However, if we only start to adopt Bitcoin in two decades later, we would be already in the Early Majority group.

Of course this is only my personal opinion; however, I also believe that those who will be born after 2070 or at least start to learn the economy at that time, will be already in the Late Majority group.

Even if they are eager to learn the technology fast, by then it will be the must, similarly to nowadays, where we all should know how to turn on a laptop.

If you can look at the consumption that spread lots faster today, still will take some time for people to adopt Bitcoin. For example, if you look at the adoption of the cell phones, it has reached 50% in 10 years, same with the internet.

However, the easiest way is to find out where we stand today, is by asking ten random people every day if they have Bitcoin or at least if they are aware of what that is.

CONSUMPTION SPREADS FASTER TODAY

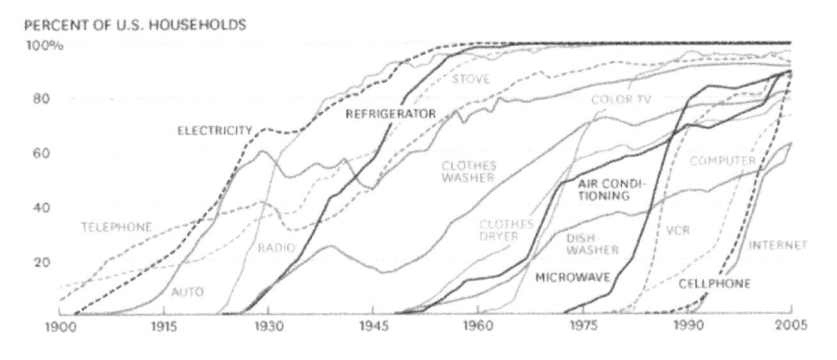

PERCENT OF U.S. HOUSEHOLDS

Chapter 7 – Potential risk of Bitcoin

Let me begin by clearing one thing. Safest and easiest way to buy Bitcoin, is not always come together. Buying Bitcoin is easy, but you always should know exactly what the risks are.

Like I mentioned before, one of my best friends wanted to start investing to Bitcoin with 1000 Euros, so I asked him:

Where do you going to keep it? He replied: Can you buy it for me? – and look after for me, please.

Well, this is not the way to go about investing your money, let me tell you right now. So, because you heard that Bitcoin is the future, and it will make a millionaire and all that, which is true by the way, does not mean that you should jump into any buy without knowing the potential risks. Let me elaborate on this.

If you have a bank card and you forget the PIN code, you can call your bank, and they will help you, or at least they should, however when it comes to Bitcoin, there is no support line to call.

Or, for example, if you choose to type your bitcoin wallet address, and you mistype it when you purchase, and the Bitcoin will get transferred to the wrong address, that's another bad news for you.

You can not call Mr. Bitcoin at Bitcoin bank and ask for a refund because you made a mistake. The reason you can not call Mr Bitcoin is this:

There is no Mr. Bitcoin, neither Bitcoin Bank. It's a decentralized digital currency, where once transactions get validated, end of story.

If you are not scared yet, then let me tell you what happens when your wallet gets hacked.

I have a friend, or I should say an associate, who has ignored to buy a cold wallet and kept his Bitcoin on his mobile application, and to be precise, he had three Bitcoin a few months back when the value of Bitcoin was between 2500 – 2700 dollars.

Yes, he got hacked, without even realizing it, and the hackers (or just one hacker) have taken all his Bitcoin, all of it is gone. So he asked me what to do.

Now let's be realistic here. You can't call the police, because they have no clue how to handle situations like that, and you can't call the Bitcoin bank either because there isn't any.

If you get hacked, and your Bitcoin disappears, you have to get on with it, and understand that it's is your fault, not the hackers.

Ok, that's not true, as it's the hackers fault too, but let me ask you one thing:

Do you leave your front door open? Or do you leave your car doors open? Maybe these examples are not close enough, but then let me ask you this:

Do you leave all your cash, dollars, pounds, euros whatever you have out to the public where anyone can grab them?

It is clearly an invitation for thieves to act upon right? For your sake, I hope you agree that your value should be secured, instead of open for anyone to grab it.

Well, if you didn't know about hackers, it's still no excuse, and still, no one will be able to help you, however, now that you know the potential risks, I am sure you agree that's better to learn how to secure your Digital currency.

In fact, step one of investing in anything, is to understand what are the potential risks.

There is no danger free business, and when it comes to Bitcoin, it's the same story.

By the way, if Bitcoin would be worthless, hackers wouldn't care about it whatsoever. However,

Hackers LOVE Bitcoin!

Hackers VS Bitcoin

Hacking used to be fun, and playground amongst techies, however as the information age has changed, hackers have grown up too.

It might have been fun to break into a Company's system and leave a trademark, so hackers can become famous online, using their aliases; however, the game has changed.

Hackers have gained superpower over the recent decade by able to access any digital information.

Not only individuals, but hacker groups have formed, and large Cybercriminals were born.

Taking it further hackers realized that stealing passports, ID-s, bank accounts, you name it, then sell them on the dark web, is not only very risky, long process, but not very profitable either.

With the Bitcoin value in the continuous increase, there is a significant demand amongst people with no technical background, hackers have learned that, there is a new market for them: Stealing Bitcoin.

You see, they don't have to take the risk of selling passports to those who might be the FBI; instead, they can steal Bitcoin and other cryptocurrencies.

Then they can transfer funds anonymously, using TOR, or even exchange them to Fiat currencies offline, using a Bitcoin ATM-s.

This is not a joke, and believe me, once your Bitcoin account get hacked, and your funds are transferred, it's game over.

There is only one way to be secured against hackers, and that is to have a cold wallet, aka hardware wallet.

I will explain in more great detail on wallet technology, as well I will recommend the best wallets in some later chapters.

Chapter 8 – LocalBitcoins

Before you run away and don't want to hear about Bitcoin anymore, let me tell you good news. You don't have to be a Chief Technology Officer to understand how to keep your Bitcoin safe.

In fact, you don't have to know about Elliptic Curve Cryptography or Discrete Logarithm Problem, or anything on how Bitcoin actually works, but you have to understand how to secure your Cryptocurrency.

Step two of investing should be to learn how to avoid potential risks by securing your investment. This brings me to another topic, and that is this:

Be aware of scammers!

There are so many ways to purchase Bitcoin, and some people come across a technique of using local Bitcoins.

You can reach the website by using the link:

https://localbitcoins.com/

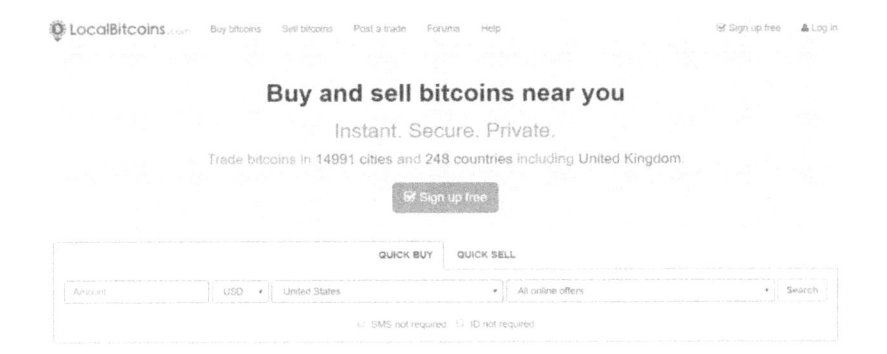

This is an attractive market where people trade cash for Bitcoin, or Bitcoin for cash; however, there are also scammers here.

Similarly, when you would buy a second hand item for example from e-Bay, you should be aware that the item might have been stolen. So, you would have to see if the seller has good feedback, ratings and so on. You have to understand that you are dealing with strangers.

So for example, if you see someone selling first time with no rating, your chances of being scammed are 50/50. What you have to understand is that if something is too good to be true, then probably is a scam.

If you see a new user on Local Bitcoins who sell at a lower rate than average people, if I were you, I wouldn't risk it, simple as that.

However, you can approach those users who are members of the site since at least 3-5 years.

That's when I would feel safe to buy, however, if someone you trust, recommends someone, that's also might be a right choice.

Those who have hundreds of reviews, you can read some of the recent ones, and decide it for yourself by understanding how trustworthy they are.

Some of these people might live locally to you, and you can meet them in person, then exchange real cash for Bitcoin, or vice versa.

Local Bitcoins is a good place to start buying Bitcoin for beginners due to its easy understanding. You can sign up for free, and the interface also has a forum, where people post questions and answers.

This is an excellent way to gain additional knowledge of the current market or anything that you have in mind.

Naturally, you can post a question, or you might go through existing threads and learn how people are talking to each other.

It's also good, as you might find someone who not only locally close to you, but you might know the person, as it has happened to another friend of mine.

Some people also post on the forum in different languages than English only, as well people share their experience with scammers as well.

- OceanWave 17m in Fraud and scam warnings
  lots of failed login attempts.
- max localbitcoins 24m in General discussion
  Do not buy referrals. It is a scam.
- dinbits 24m in General discussion
  Useless thread 02-22-2015
- kdot123 in General discussion Spam
  someone want to send me a bitcoin, should i send my user name to receive?
- CADSSELLA 36m in Fraud and scam warnings
  scammer account :JeckieWang
- vaehsmama31410 47m in General discussion
  Davmoney.club
- ahsanmastoi 1h in General discussion
  Bitcoin buying / selling in karachi
- opticbit 1h in Fraud and scam warnings
  paypal chargeback on other site
- scottemick 1h in General discussion
  USPS tracking down

However before you would buy Bitcoin from anyone, you must have a wallet.

Chapter 9 – Hot wallets

My recommendation is to read this book and learn more before you buy any Bitcoin. However, It's time to understand the wallet technology. First, I would like to point out that there is a misconception, or I should say misunderstanding what the crypto wallet is.

Many people believe when purchasing Bitcoin, it will be stored on the wallet. This is not true. Bitcoin that you will purchase will be recorded on the blockchain, in fact, all Bitcoin that ever was mined, and will be mined, are always going to stay on the Blockchain.

Bitcoin has no physical presence, and when you are transferring Bitcoin, you don't move the Digital coins anywhere; instead, you assign a new wallet address to the amount of Bitcoin you buy or sell. Wallets are a software technology, which stores your private and public keys, and interacts with the Blockchain to allow you to access your Bitcoin account.

Once you have access to your account, you can send, receive, or directly monitor your balance. There are many different kinds of wallets, and some portfolios support different currencies, however, some only supports one particular crypto currency. For example, imagine that you have an HSBC bank card that you can access your Euros; however, you also have another card with Bank of America to obtain your dollars. When it comes to a crypto currency wallet, some wallets can support multiple currencies simultaneously.

Online wallet

You might choose to have a wallet from Blockchain.info that allows you to have access to your Bitcoin as well Ether. By the way I have a Blockchain wallet, in fact, that was my first wallet, and I still have it, even it's limited for currencies, I still use it, and recommend to anyone to start with it.

You can have a blockchain wallet for free on your desktop as well on your smart phone by reaching the website called: blockchain.info

Once you enter the site, you can click on the menu: wallet, then click on: Get started now. That will take you to the registration page, where you can sign up in no time, and buy Bitcoin very quickly.

You can link your current bank account and start to purchase your first Bitcoin. This is how I bought my first Bitcoin, and I would highly recommend it for beginners.

It's effortless to use it, and start using your first Bitcoin wallet. This wallet does not support all the currencies that you might want to invest in the future. However right now the focus is on purchasing Bitcoin, or even before that, to have your first crypto currency wallet that supports Bitcoin.

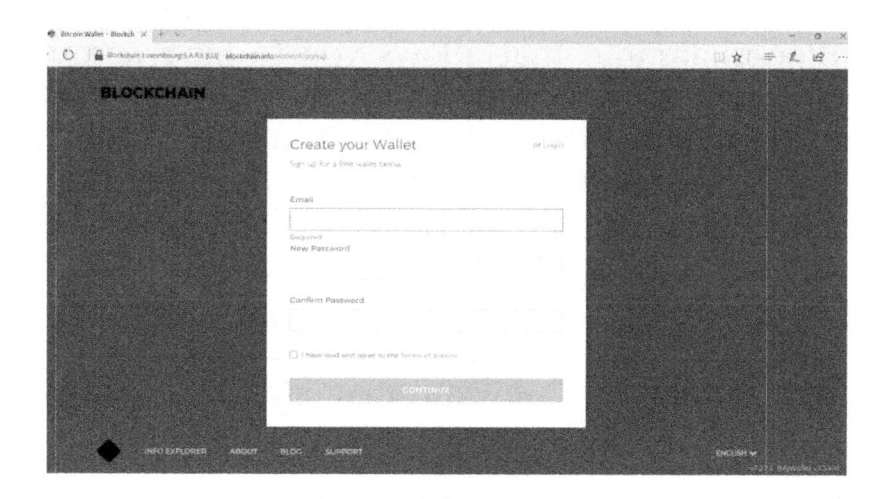

If you start with a Blockchain wallet, which I highly recommend, do not go crazy and invest all your money. Instead, have a feel for the technology, and start with 100 dollars. Some people recommend no more than 500 dollars as a first investment, however, if you are a complete beginner, you can do even just 50 dollars worth for the first time. When I have started, I went in with 100 dollars. When you link your bank account, the options to purchase Bitcoin for 50 dollars, the fees seemed to be higher than buying for 100 dollars worth, so I have chosen to have 100 dollars as my first investment.

As I mentioned before, easy does not come with safety, and it is also true with a Blockchain wallet. For instance, if Blockchain.info gets hacked, the hackers can take control all wallets that reside on their platform.

It had happened before with other trading companies, which resulted in administration; therefore you have to understand, that any online platform exists today is never 100% secured.

Also, once you have a wallet installed on your mobile phone or desktop computer, those devices also can be hacked.

I am not saying that once you buy Bitcoin, you will be hacked in the same day, but there is a potential risk, and you have to live with that.

Of course, if you back up your wallet, you have a better chance of being able to retrieve your funds, in case something bad happens.

Desktop wallets

Desktop wallets are reasonably secured; however, they can only be used on your desktop computer.

Once you have installed it on a particular computer or laptop, that will be your only device where you can access your Bitcoin or other cryptocurrencies.

As I mentioned before, it is not based in the cloud, and if you regularly turn off your pc, and having an antivirus, you should be just fine.

Of course, there are many ways for hackers to get hold of your desktop wallet using various phishing attacks, or viruses from drive by download sites or torrent websites.

Once the hackers would access your private keys, they would be able to access your digital currencies; therefore, it is not recommended for long term use, or even for short term for large sums of coins.

Again, desktop wallets are easy to be downloaded, as well to be used, however still not fully secured.

Mobile wallets

There are many different mobile wallets, and Blockchain.info has one as well. However, Blockchain.info provides both, online and desktop wallets.

On the other hand, there are some mobile wallets, specifically for cell phones. Having a mobile wallet is essential for making payments anywhere you go, as your cell phone probably will be with you most of the times.

Mobile wallets can provide good security too; however, you must back up your mobile wallet too, same as your desktop wallet.

For example, if you would lose your phone or break it, buying another phone and having backup phrases for your mobile wallet, you can simply back up your new cell phone, like nothing happened.

Again, if you don't back up your mobile wallet, you can lose access to all your Bitcoin forever.

Chapter 10 – Cold wallets

Cold wallets aka Hardware wallets, those two descriptions are often used both, and really means the same thing. One of these devices, is what you must have if you planning on purchasing large sums of Bitcoin.

These are the best and safest wallets that you can have. Hackers can't do much by attacking it from online, as the cold wallets are keeping the private keys on the hardware, away from the internet.

Some of these wallets, are often look like a USB Stick, and unfortunately, people believe that having a USB stick is the same as having a cold or hardware wallet. This is not true.

USB stick cannot be backed up; neither understands the current market. Of course, hardware wallets do look like USB devices. Hardware wallets also have to be connected to the internet for sending or receiving funds. However, this would require a special USB type of cable.

Any cryptocurrency that you are afraid to keep it on a mobile or online wallet, you should keep them on a cold wallet.

There is no way to someone hack your cold wallet, unless they have physical access to it. However, still they must break your pin code, then must have access to your secret keys that you write down on a piece of paper when you use the device first time.

The only downside, in my opinion, is that if you want to sell some of your Bitcoin quickly, you can not. I mean if you have your cold wallet with you, and there is a desktop pc around, then it can be done in less than 5 minutes.

However, when you have a mobile wallet, transaction can take like 10-15 seconds. Traders always have lot's of Bitcoin on their mobile wallets too in case it's time to sell or buy.

I call myself an investor, when it comes to Bitcoin or any other cryptocurrency. I do believe that Bitcoin will continuously increase in it's value, and while it does, Fiat currencies will steadily decrease in value; therefore it will provide an additional boost to the value of Bitcoin to grow even stronger.

Hardware wallets are the most secured, there is no doubt about that, however at first, it can be difficult to understand how cold wallets work.

Once you receive a cold wallet, at first you have to create your Pin code. Next, it will ask you if you are backing up an existing account, or creating a new wallet.

So choosing to build a new portfolio, it will generate 24 worlds that you have to write down on a piece of paper which comes with the wallet.

This is also known as a seed recovery sheet. Once that complete, you have to update the firmware. That could take another five to ten minutes.

After that, you have to choose what type of cryptocurrency wallets you want to download on your wallet. Hardware wallets such as Trezor or Ledger Nano S can support five different crypto wallets at the same time.

Of course you can choose from more than five currencies, however, let me give you an example: Let's say that you want to have Bitcoin, Litecoin, Monero, Dash, Zcash, which is not a problem.

However, a week later you want to add another crypto wallet to your hardware wallet, for example, Ethereum, you will not be able to do so until you delete one of the existing crypto wallets.

So, there are pros and cons to it, however to setup a cold wallet you might require to allocate 30-40 minutes for these purposes. Installing a mobile wallet is less than a minute; but you have to respect the security that comes with a hardware wallet.

Additionally, if you lose your equipment or get it broken, you might choose to purchase another one, and having those 24 random words you have previously wrote down, you can re-install all your crypto wallets in no time.

A cold wallet is an absolute must to have, especially if you thinking of a long term investment in Crypto, like I do.

Even I keep on telling you that you must have a cold wallet, there are few other cons that you should be aware of, or you should prepare to.

First is this: Do not keep the recovery sheet at the same place where you keep the hardware. Why is that?

Imagine that you get a burglary, and they find a cryptocurrency hardware wallet, and next to it another piece of paper that says: Recovery sheet, and below the 24 words that you wrote down.

They don't even have to take your hardware wallet. All they need is a recovery map, as they can recover your wallet, using another device that is compatible with the one you have.

As you see, even it is the most secure wallet that exists; still, all can be lost by not taking extra measures.

Let's take another example. This time there is a fire in the building. Again it is good to have a recovery sheet, however, if that gets lost for any reason, well, if you still have the device, you have two choices. One is to look after that device forever, or send every fund to another device that is backed up, and you know exactly where that recovery sheet is.

You might choose to put it somewhere safe like in the cloud, so you can access it even in the future at any time, however having all those 24 words together not such a good idea, especially keeping them online.

So what you can do is this: Keep six words on Evernote, another six notes on Facebook, another six on Gmail, and another six on Yahoo storage. This is just an idea.

However, it's completely up to you but let me tell you another issue with too much security. I will assume that you are men, and you have a wife, who isn't really into the crypto world like you.

Most probably your wife has no clue what Bitcoin is, not to mention hardware wallets, or recovery sheets, and platform exchanges.

Let's imagine that you have 10 Bitcoin and each Bitcoin worth around 4000 dollars, but something happens to you. Let's say that you end up in the hospital in the coma.

I am sorry that I come up with the worse examples, but my point is this.

There is no sense to save all that crypto money for your son or wife, if they never going to be able to access it.

So, because you put the recovery sheet in 4 different safes, and each safe is in various banks, and each bank is in various country, you might choose to have so much security that not only hackers, but even your loved ones won't be able to access those funds ever.

What I am trying to explain is that you should teach your loved ones, or you should tell them that you have written down everything step-by-step, how to access those funds, in case of emergency.

Probably not everyone will do that. However, I think it's worth to mention to you, so you can decide how to go about it.

Chapter 11 – Wallet recommendation

Some questions that you might want to ask yourself before choosing a wallet:

- Do you need a wallet so you can use it all the time, every day?
- Do you need a wallet so you can keep on buying crypto currency and   holding it for long a time?
- Do you need multiple currencies or only Bitcoin?
- Do you want anytime access, or only sometimes?
- Do you want to get paid in Bitcoin?

Once you have settled and understood your need, you can choose what best fit your requirements, then go for the wallet suits you best. That's being said lets late a look at what I recommend that is a must have.

Hot wallet recommendations

Blockchain

I have explained already how Blockchain wallet works, and its limitations when it comes to cryptocurrencies. However, this is my number 1 recommendation to those, who are entirely new to Bitcoin and other cryptocurrencies. The platform can be reached on blockchain.info

JAXX

Jaxx is one of the most popular mobile wallet, and to be honest, everyone's favourite.

Jaxx supports multicurrencies, such as Bitcoin, Ethereum, Ethereum Classic, Litecoin, DASH, Zcash, Monero. Jaxx supports 9 different platforms, that including Windows, Apple and Linux desktop, Android, IOS mobile and tablet, Google Chrome and Firefox extensions as well.
Jaxx has an excellent user interface that gives you comfortable easy to understand, easy to use experience.

Having on multiple devices, it synchronizes to another devices too, same as Blockchain wallet does. Jaxx appears to be slow sometimes, however this could be, because it is not open source, and it supports multiple currencies.
Jaxx can be found at: jaxx.io

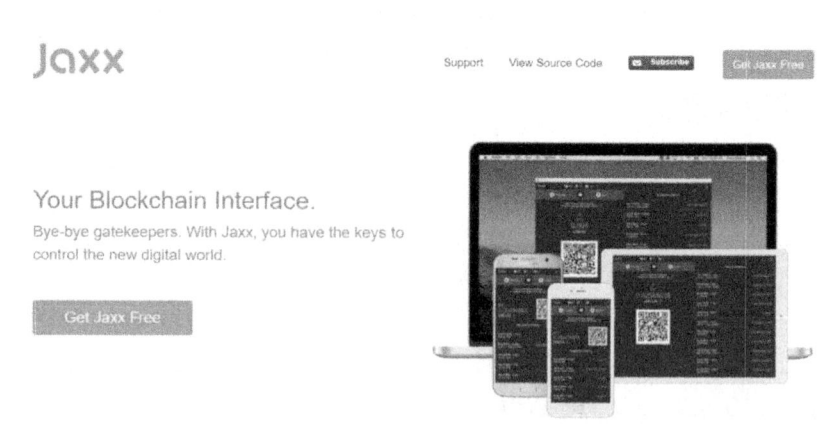

Cold wallet recommendations

TREZOR

Trezor is a hardware wallet, that currently one of the best in terms of security. It is an excellent cold wallet, especially to store Bitcoin on it.

Once you have a Trezor, you will know why it is so secured as it has a screen, that only you can see. I mean, the Trezor screen is not visible on your computer, therefore, hackers can't get to it, and your private keys are completely off line.

The interface is very easy to use, and I would recommend it to anyone. It also have a web interface for easier use, however the screen is built in to provide additional security.

If you want to buy it from the source, you can buy one on following the link:

https://trezor.io/

It's open source, therefore if case you lose it, you can buy another one, or similar device that supports the same functions, then back it up very quickly.

It only costs 89 Euros, however, when I bought it, I have also purchased a Cable for an Android phone, and paid for DHL shipping another 26 Euros

Then I got charged 21% VAT, so instead of 89 euro, somehow I had to pay 145.20 Euros in the end.

I am not saying they are scammers, they are not, but you will get charged for postage no matter where you order from, and the VAT itself was 25.2 Euros, which I wasn't happy about either.

Anyways, it is coming from the Chech Republic, and if you live there, you might not require paying the VAT, but I wouldn't count on that.

As I mentioned earlier, it is not a scam, and it is a must have, however before you consider buying one, make sure that you are aware of additional charges.

In case you don't believe me, I have taken a screenshot of my order, and as you can see, I have ordered a White color.

You have two options when it comes to the color choices: Black or white.

Another issue that was not in my favor is when I bought it, there was a warning message that it would take six weeks for delivery.

However, once you move on, and click on payments, you have options for DHL delivery that is between 3 to 5 days costing 26 euros, or traditional delivery that is 4-8 weeks for 12 Euros.

So I have chosen the DHL, as I wanted to store all my Bitcoin on a secure wallet as soon as possible.

Still, after six working days have passed, I have sent them an email asking them what is happening.

They replied that there is a warning message about the delivery that takes at least six weeks.

I was outraged, and my point was that if it's six weeks as a minimum to deliver, then why do they still offer 3 to 5 days DHL delivery.

In the end I got it after five weeks; however it is a long waiting time, but again it is a must have, so it's all right.

I have survived all the waiting, and my Blockchain wallet didn't get hacked while I did it.

Still, I would recommend to buy a cold storage wallet first, only then start buying Bitcoin, especially in large quantities.

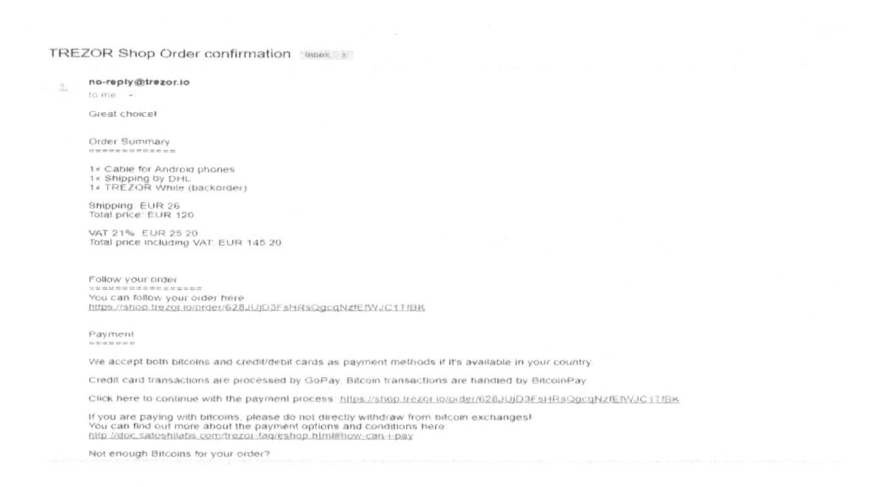

Ledger Nano S

Ledger Nano was no different when it comes to delivery, I had to wait 5 weeks, and few more days too.

The difference was that the Ledger Nano S was only 69.60 Euro and it's already including TAX. Of course, I had to pay for the postage another 16,28 Euros, this time for UPS. Totalling the full payment of 85,88 Euros. To buy it from the source, just follow the link:

https://www.ledgerwallet.com/r/e101

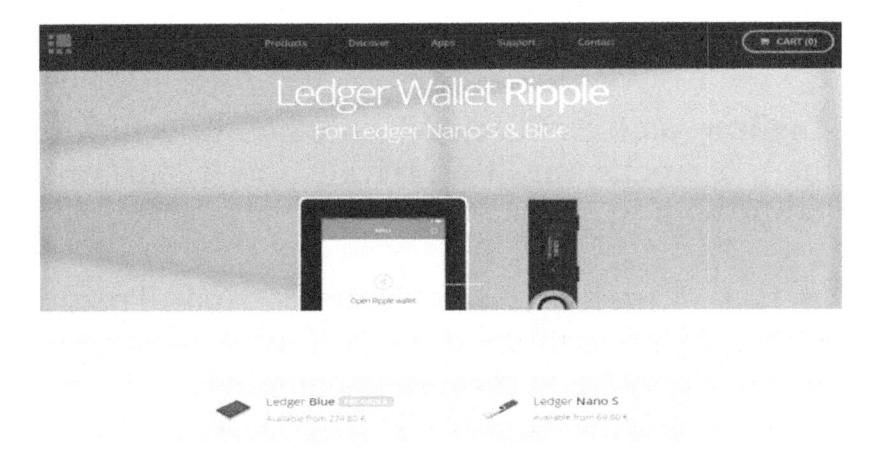

Ledger Nano had another trick, and that is this: Once I made the payment, I got a confirmation e-mail, stating this:

Due to a very high level of demand, and in accordance to the delivery terms you accepted at ordering time by checking the confirmation box, your order will not be shipped before September 4, 2017 and then will be delivered to your address 2-5 days later.

Now bare in mind this was back in June 24th of 2017, meaning I should wait 11 weeks for delivery. I was really sad, and for some reason I can not recall any checkbox when I first ordered one.

However, since I have ordered another one for my father, this time I got them checkboxes for sure.

Anyhow, as I mentioned I only had to wait less then 6 weeks for it's arrival, and I am vary happy with it.

In fact, I prefer Ledger Nano S, than Trezor. Ledger Nano is much more beautiful, at least to me, and it's screen is more likeable.

It's also cheaper, and the knowledge is pretty much the same as the Trezor. When it comes to the build quality, also the Ledger Nano is what I would recommend.

The ledger Nano S has a capability to take a weight of a car, so my first choice is Ledger Nano S

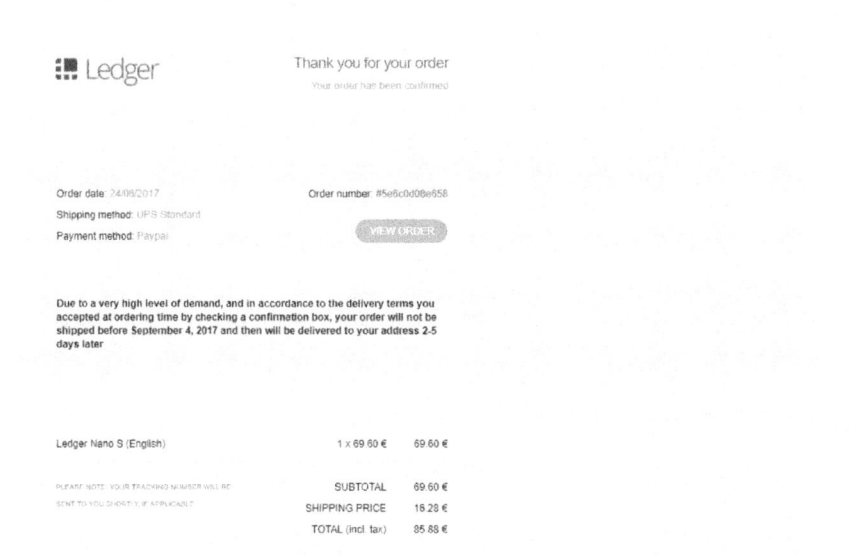

My recommendation is to use a cold wallet, so you can not be hacked, and again, as I mentioned before, I would recommend to go for Ledger Nano S.

https://www.ledgerwallet.com/r/e101

Not only because it is cheaper, but it is not that scammy like Trezor, where you have additional VAT fees and super expensive, also the Ledger Nano looks much more better, but in the same time I have them both Trezor as well Ledger Nano S.

Integration using Ledger Nano S

Ledger Nano S also compatible with another nine different Cryptocurrency software wallets, that can integrate as below:

- Ledger Wallet Bitcoin
- Ledger Wallet Ethereum
- Ledger Wallet Ripple
- Copay
- Electrum
- Mycelium
- MyEtherWallet
- GreenBits
- BitGo

Ledger Wallet Bitcoin	Ledger Wallet Ethereum	Ledger Wallet Ripple
Copay	Electrum	Mycelium
MyEtherWallet	GreenBits	BitGo

This is the best wallet I can recommend, however I wanted you to know that are other options too. Once again, you should decide it for your own reasons first, then you will be able to make the best choice for yourself. Again, there are many wallets that you can use for free right away, and you probably should as your first wallet. However, when it comes to investing, hot wallets are not safe, therefore I would only recommend a low amount like 100 dollars as your first investment.

Anything less then 500 dollars are not that attractive for Hackers, however it doesn't mean that you are safe, therefore only invest in the amount of Bitcoin as much as you are ready to lose, in case you get hacked.

In the meanwhile, you can buy a Ledger Nano S, as it will take few weeks to arrive, and while you are waiting, you can read more books on Blockchain and Bitcoin for better understanding, as well to become more comfortable with the technology.

Once you receive your Ledger Nano S, you can start to invest larger amounts, and keep it safe on your Ledger Nano S.

https://www.ledgerwallet.com/r/e101

I have both Trezor as well Ledger Nano, and I also know that some people prefer Trezor over the Ledger, however in my opinion, Ledger Nano S is the best.

Trezor was released in 2013 and it's design doesn't look so appealing, however Ledger Nano S was released in 2016, with a lot better looking hardware, or at least to me, it is more stylish then the Trezor.

I believe that Ledger Nano S has a way better looking then Trezor, however if you think otherwise, it's fine, but please bare in mind that Trezor is more expensive.

In order to buy them again use the following links:

Trezor:
https://trezor.io/

Ledger Nano S:
https://www.ledgerwallet.com/r/e101

As I mentioned, I had to wait for both of them, however if you do not want to wait for weeks, you can check on eBay or Amazon where others might sell it too.

I have realized that second hand devices are much more expensive. In the same time, it might worth it.

What I mean is first I have tried to buy it on Amazon, even it was more expensieve by a third party seller, still I was going to buy it from Amazon, as I trust Amazon delivery, their customer service as well it's fast.

I have Amazon Prime too, and pretty much anything I order from Amazon, I do get it as a next day delivery.

So the problem was when I wanted to buy the Ledger Nano S is simply was the availability. Literally Amazon was out of stock too, so, even I was going to pay more for the Ledger, next day delivery would have been awesome, but no stock.

If you are in the rush, or just want to use Hardware wallet right away, like I wanted to, I would advise to check Amazon first, as you may get it lot more faster if they have in stock of course.

Chapter 12 – Bitcoin ATM-s

That's right, there are machines called Bitcoin ATM-s. They are connected to the internet, as well looking very similar to a traditional ATM-s.

However the purpose of these are to convert Bitcoin to Fiat currency or vice versa. In 2013 the first Bitcoin ATM has been installed in Canada, and it has been a continuous increase of Bitcoin ATM-s ever since. Currently, as of 2017 August, there are 1493 Bitcoin ATM-s around the world, operating in 57 different Countries.

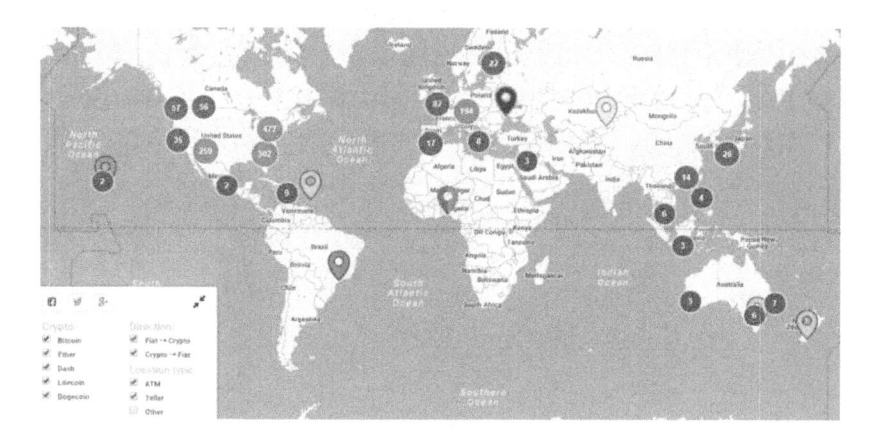

Types of Bitcoin ATM-s

It worth to mention that are many different types of Bitcoin ATM-s, and some are only operate in one way, however, some has a two-way function. It also depends where you use the Bitcoin ATM-s , as if you want to convert your existing Bitcoin to cash, you will probably receive the local currency of that country.

Other issues that you might encounter is the fees. There are Bitcoin ATM-s that are operating with no fees, however some others can take as much as 5-10% fees once used.

The legacy of Bitcoin is that are no fees, however, there are many operators who paid for producing such machines, as well costs to pay the electricity bills, rental fees, therefore some might charge for a certain fee.

It is advisable to check the fees before using one, however the comfort that it provides are extremely helpful.

How to use Bitcoin ATM-s

In case you wonder how it works, I can tell you from experience that is relatively easy.

Let's assume that you want to buy some Bitcoin, using traditional Cash such as dollar. The checklist that you should have is this:

• Smart phone with internet connectivity: Any types of smart phones are ok.
• Hot wallet downloaded on the smart phone: Blockchain wallet or Jaxx
• Dollar bill: Ten, twenty or any dollar bill that you want to convert into Bitcoin.
• Bitcoin ATM near you: You can find a local Bitcoin ATM near you by visiting this link:

https://coinatmradar.com/

Once you have downloaded one of the wallets I have recommended, or any other Cryptocurrency wallet to your smart phone, visit a local Bitcoin ATM.

In case you think that Bitcoin ATM-s are placed in some dark hidden street, let me tell you that normally the Bitcoin ATM-s are in a public place such as restaurants, pubs, or local shops, places that are many people visit daily.

Buy Bitcoin
Once you are there, and happy with the fees that the ATM will operate, do the following:

Step 1. Click on the machine's screen: Buy Bitcoin

Step 2. Open your Hot wallet on your smart phone, and select: receive. This will bring up your QR code on your smart phone screen.

Step 3. Hold your phone to the Bitcoin ATM-s screen, and let it scan your QR Code.
In the meanwhile the ATM will tell you to insert a bill.

Step 4. Feed the paper bill to the machine. This time you can feed as much as Bitcoin is available, however if you do it first time, you might try it only with a 10 dollar bill.

Step 5. Click send Bitcoin on the ATM. The Bitcoin ATM will perform the transaction, and you might see on the screen something like: Sending Bitcoin. It would take around less then a second.

Step 6. Check your smart phone for notifications: You should have on your screen something like: New payment received. Of course it depends on what wallet you are using. Once you happy with the Bitcoin that you have received, you may also try out how to sell your Bitcoin for cash. Again, you should check beforehand, making sure that you visit a two-way function Bitcoin ATM, but of course if you only want to buy Bitcoin, than you can visit a one way operating Bitcoin ATM too.

This case let's assume that you are ready to convert your Bitcoin to cash, using a Bitcoin ATM. Please note that some of the Bitcon ATM-s are the minimum limit is at least 5 dollars, meaning if you only want to sell Bitcoin that worth only one dollar, it might not be possible. It is better to check before, however normally the minimum cash to take out, is at least 5 dollars.

Sell Bitcoin

Step 1. On the Bitcoin ATM, select: I want Cash. This will bring up the next screen, listing 5, 20, 50 that you can tap on. Note here: some ATM-s have the same functions like traditional ATM-s where there is an option for: Select other amounts, however some Bitcoin ATM-s have no numbers to create your special amounts, instead, you can keep taping on the listed amounts. For example if you want 30 dollars, but there is only option for 5, 10 and 20, you can tap on the 10 three times. This will provide you with a 30 dollars.

Step 2. Choose the amount you want: For example, select 5, for five dollars worth of Bitcoin.

Step 3. Tap on the next screen: Cash out. Once you tap on: Cash out, the ATM will generate a QR code. This will be for you to scan it, using your smart phone.

Step 4. On your smart phone, open the hot wallet and select send.

Step 5. Hold your smart phone to the ATM and scan the QR code that the ATM has generated previously.

Once you have scanned the QR code, using your smart phone, it will generate the transaction that you will have to confirm in the next step.

This step, your phone will calculate the amount of Bitcoin that you have to send to the Bitcoin ATM's address.

Step 6. On your smart phone, select: SEND. Once you tap on SEND on your smart phone, it will ask you to confirm it again by opening another window.
Here, you will see how much Bitcoin you will send to the address of the ATM.

Step 7. Select: Confirm. This will send the transaction to the ATM. This will take another second or two. However once complete, the Bitcoin ATM will come up with a screen: Bitcoin received! > This screen will quickly change to another display where it will say: Dispensing... Please take your cash.

Step 8. Take your cash! Check on the Bitcoin ATM below for your cash, and take it. There are many different Bitcoin ATM-s and some functions different then others, however the process is somewhat the similar.

I have not try them all, however I did try out two of them already and they both were working just fine. I have tried one that was charging me for 3% and another Bitcoin ATM that had no fee.

In the end of the day, for the convenience of selling and buying Bitcoin instantly, and anonymously it's awesome.

In case you are afraid of being hacked online, this is one of the safest way to buy Bitcoin. Again, I am not sure where you live, however using coin atm radar, you should be able to find one close by to your home or work.

https://coinatmradar.com/

Chapter 13 – Best Online Trading platforms

Back in the day you were lucky if you were able to find at least one Bitcoin trading platform. However, nowadays, there are so many that you cant even count them. The real problem is not to find one, instead making sure that you are not getting scammed on some fake cryptocurrency trading platform.

I will explain with more details on how to recognize fake websites and scammers on the next chapter, however first I would like to introduce some great platforms that you can use in the future.

Please note, this book has been written in August 2017, and I am pointing out the best online trading platforms that are exist today.

Instead of analysing each online trading platform, the question you should ask is this: how to find genuine online trading platforms without getting scammed.

In order to find platforms, as a starting point, you should be looking at cryptocurrencies that are on the market since years such as Bitcoin. Bitcoin is not a scam, in fact Bitcoin is the strongest cryptocurrency of all, and of course the first even cryptocurrency that was created. Bitcoin exists since 2009 January, meaning more then 8 years already on the market and stronger than ever.

Of course you already know that by now, however just to point it out again, if you follow Bitcoin and it's markets, by what platforms it is mainly traded, you should be able to find those online trading platforms that are completely legit. Where to start?

The platform that you are looking for is what I already introduced previously that is called:

coinmarketcap.com

#	Name	Symbol	Market Cap	Price	Circulating Supply	Volume (24h)	% 1h	% 24h	% 7d
1	Bitcoin	BTC	$72,341,504,692	$4376.85	16,528,212	$1,499,450,000	-0.41%	0.78%	6.30%
2	Ethereum	ETH	$32,003,460,344	$339.45	94,279,504	$552,367,000	-0.33%	1.96%	14.04%
3	Bitcoin Cash	BCH	$10,118,435,034	$611.46	16,548,100	$390,579,000	-0.95%	-2.72%	-16.64%
4	Ripple	XRP	$7,756,499,087	$0.202288	38,343,841,883 *	$191,742,000	-0.75%	-5.53%	27.11%
5	Litecoin	LTC	$3,351,209,950	$63.64	52,654,807	$830,264,000	1.36%	23.21%	36.32%
6	Dash	DASH	$2,714,728,085	$361.12	7,517,828	$146,426,000	-0.53%	-5.08%	22.71%
7	IOTA	MIOTA	$2,553,337,668	$0.918622	2,779,530,283 *	$19,009,000	-0.04%	-4.18%	-6.04%
8	NEM	XEM	$2,479,500,000	$0.275500	8,999,999,999 *	$8,221,800	-1.39%	1.91%	-1.01%

https://coinmarketcap.com/all/views/all/

Once you have navigated to coinmarketcap, you will find all cryptocurrencies that are on the market. Next if you click on Bitcoin, it will take you to the next page, where you can find more details about the currency:

In this page there many information that you can find about Bitcoin, including:

- All the websites where you can find out more information.
- Market capitalizations,
- Additional tools,
- Historical Data, and so on...

It's easy to just get lost here, as there are some great information about Bitcoin, however, our main focus is to find a genuine online trading platform, therefore you should carry on by selecting the menu called: Markets:

By selecting the menu option: Markets, the new window will open where you can find information about:

• All Bitcoin Markets,
• Source – these are the platforms we are looking for.
• Pair – meaning what Bitcoin can be exchanged into.
• Price – This is the price of the Bitcoin on each of those markets

• Volume – This number represents the percentage of all Bitcoin that is currently on the market; however the number is unique to each platform.

You can also find on the right another button that now shows USD, however, if you click on it, you should see all other currencies that you can trade with when trading Bitcoin.

Bitcoin Markets

#	Source	Pair	Volume (24h)	Price	Volume (%)
1	Bitfinex	BTC/USD	$49,390,000	$4353.10	3.30%
2	Bittrex	LSK/BTC	$49,307,300	$4496.61	3.29%
3	Poloniex	LTC/BTC	$49,068,500	$4378.42	3.27%
4	HitBTC	BCC/BTC	$43,728,500	$4357.28	2.92%
5	Poloniex	XMR/BTC	$39,975,400	$4323.34	2.67%
6	Bithumb	BTC/KRW	$35,357,600	$4378.48	2.36%
7	OKCoin.cn	BTC/CNY	$33,581,100	$4358.69	2.24%
8	Poloniex	LSK/BTC	$31,004,500	$4436.32	2.07%
9	BTCC	BTC/CNY	$30,510,900	$4353.54	2.04%
10	Poloniex	XRP/BTC	$29,447,100	$4315.15	1.96%
11	Huobi	BTC/CNY	$29,156,300	$4345.86	1.95%
12	Bittrex	MCO/BTC	$28,997,300	$4437.16	1.93%
13	Poloniex	ETH/BTC	$28,678,600	$4360.14	1.91%
14	GDAX	BTC/USD	$28,249,300	$4368.00	1.88%
15	Bittrex	LTC/BTC	$27,278,600	$4378.73	1.82%
16	bitFlyer	BTC/JPY	$22,569,200	$4371.36	1.51%

At this moment Bitfinex has the most Bitcoin on the market, and it's pairing BTC/USD, meaning you can buy Bitcoin to US dollar or vice versa.

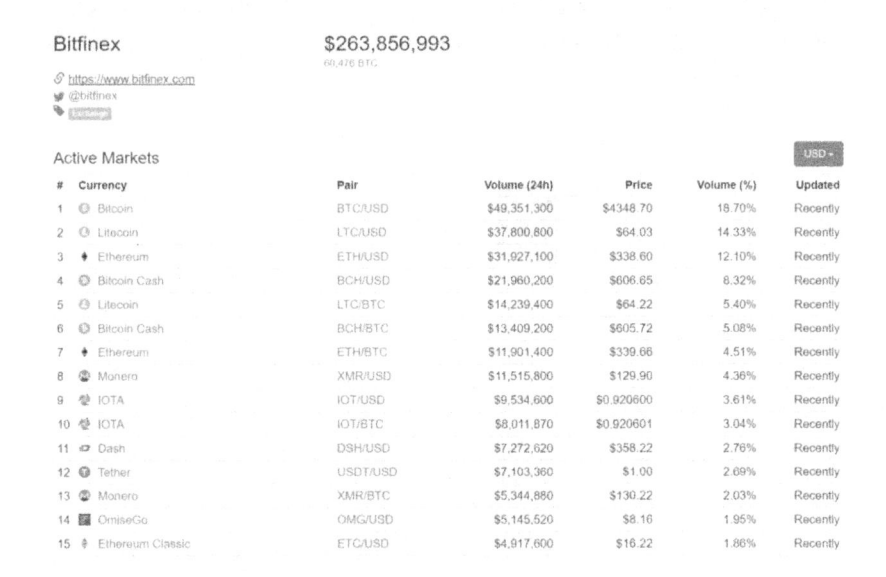

Bitfinex — $263,856,993 (60,476 BTC)

https://www.bitfinex.com
@bitfinex

Active Markets

#	Currency	Pair	Volume (24h)	Price	Volume (%)	Updated
1	Bitcoin	BTC/USD	$49,351,300	$4348.70	18.70%	Recently
2	Litecoin	LTC/USD	$37,800,800	$64.03	14.33%	Recently
3	Ethereum	ETH/USD	$31,927,100	$338.60	12.10%	Recently
4	Bitcoin Cash	BCH/USD	$21,960,200	$606.65	8.32%	Recently
5	Litecoin	LTC/BTC	$14,239,400	$64.22	5.40%	Recently
6	Bitcoin Cash	BCH/BTC	$13,409,200	$605.72	5.08%	Recently
7	Ethereum	ETH/BTC	$11,901,400	$339.66	4.51%	Recently
8	Monero	XMR/USD	$11,515,800	$129.90	4.36%	Recently
9	IOTA	IOT/USD	$9,534,600	$0.920600	3.61%	Recently
10	IOTA	IOT/BTC	$8,011,870	$0.920601	3.04%	Recently
11	Dash	DSH/USD	$7,272,620	$358.22	2.76%	Recently
12	Tether	USDT/USD	$7,103,360	$1.00	2.69%	Recently
13	Monero	XMR/BTC	$5,344,880	$130.22	2.03%	Recently
14	OmiseGo	OMG/USD	$5,145,520	$8.16	1.95%	Recently
15	Ethereum Classic	ETC/USD	$4,917,600	$16.22	1.86%	Recently

Next by clicking on Bitfinex, it will take you over to the next page, where you can see all the currencies that this site is currently trading with, as well the website on the top right corner, and its Twitter account:

By clicking on their twitter account, you can see how much engagement the site has. Twitter has all the complaints as well appreciation for the platform, therefore by taking a quick look for educational purposes, is a good idea.

For example, you can see that are more than 56.8K followers, and that can tell you lots too. If it was a new trading platform, you would probably see lot fewer members, and that case would be advisable not to get involved yet;

however more than 50K followers are just fine. Also you can contact others and ask their opinion about the platform.

Of course this is a genuine platform; therefore you can also visit their website at the link provided on coinmarketcap:

https://www.bitfinex.com/

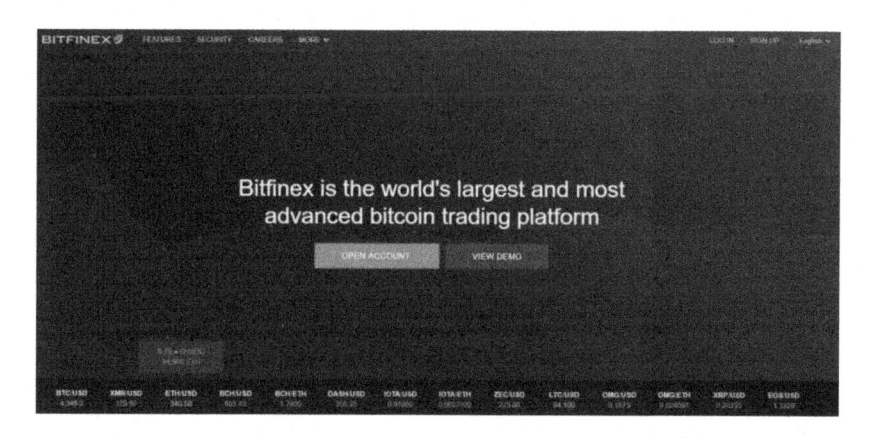

Once you have reached the platform, you can just register for free, and start trading Bitcoin or other cryptocurrencies. Bitfinex is one the most respected Online Trading platform for multiple reasons.

Unfortunately, Bitfinex was hacked in 2016 August, and some of the traders also have lost their value, as some of them have left their cryptocurrencies on the platform instead saving them to a hardware wallet.

The hackers have taken 120K Bitcoin at the time, and even it seemed that Bitfinex would go into administration like some other crypto traders previously, Bitfinex has recovered.

In fact not only recovered, but paid in full to all their traders who have lost their value when the hack has happened.

Even it has taken eight months for them to reimburse all their investors, they could have just closed their doors, however instead they have looked after their investors, and paid back all their losses in full in 2017 April.

Since that event, there have been even more investors than ever, as they have provided an example of trust and long term relationship, when it comes to investing in cryptocurrencies.

I wanted to show you an example on how to find an online trading platform by only following links, however, as you can see there are many platforms to choose from.

Because of that fact, I will cover some other platforms that I have been using previously.

First things first, even Bitfinex have paid back all their investors, which is nice. Still, I hope you understood by now, that no online trading platform is safe. They all can be hacked, and probably will be hacked some day.

Because of the way that cryptocurrency works, there is very little that police can do, if they might take away all your Bitcoin.

Simply, there is no guarantee that once these platforms are hacked, they will give you back all your losses.

Coinbase

Coinbase is one of the most convenient exchanges out there to invest in, or withdraw money if you live in the US or other supported countries. The website works just perfectly, and you can reach it by following this link:

https://www.coinbase.com/?locale=en

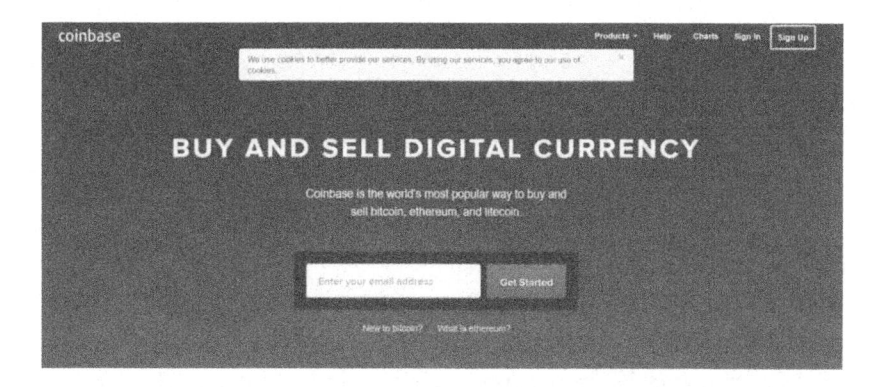

The interface is user-friendly, and it is recommended to anyone, even if you have no technical background, you will be able to navigate the site quickly.

Additionally, they have some excellent charts to see when it comes to technical analysis. If you have a problem, you can log a support ticket, and the responses are usually speedy.

Coinbase is also a good place for beginners, however when it comes to authentication, you should make sure that you choose to have a google authenticator, instead of getting verified by MMS.

Using MMS to authenticate is one of the ways that your account can be hacked. Therefore it is highly recommended to take the right security measurements.

Poloniex

The site can be reached by clicking on the link:

https://poloniex.com/

Poloniex has countless of crypto currencies; however the highest volume of exchanges are Bitcoin and Ethereum. This site does not except

US dollars; instead you must use Tether, that is another crypto currency which has a purpose of a US dollar. Meaning 1 tether is always around 1 dollar. On Tether, you can find more information on their website:

https://tether.to/

Tether is a digital value of the dollar. However, some online platforms such as Poloniex do not want to trade with the traditional dollar, instead tether.

Back to Poloniex, they have become so overwhelmed due to too many investors; they are literally super busy for the next few years probably.

What you have to understand is that, when you register on Poloniex, they will check your account, and eventually verify it before they allow you to trade on their platform. Now that's all ok; however, they have so many new customers recently, that some people have been waiting three months to get verified.

However, some others don't even get replied after three months. The customer service became horrible over the last six months, and many people have just moved on and started trading on other platforms instead.

Kraken

Kraken can be used for those living in the European Union countries. Reaching Kraken, only use the link:

https://www.kraken.com/

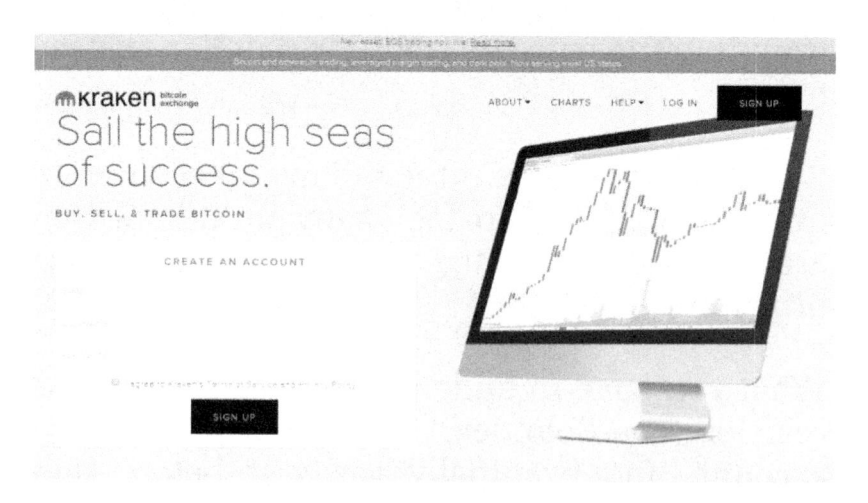

Kraken accepts Euro as well British pounds; therefore it's one of the best choices to Europeans to trade on.

Kraken uses a Tier system, meaning you can start trading as a Tier 1, where you can exchange between all currencies, but account funding is limited to digital currencies only.

Tier 2, is where your daily limit is 2000 dollars worth by both, depositing, or withdrawing, and in both, Fiat currencies as well in cryptocurrencies.

Tier 3, it allows the same functions as Tier 2, however this time the daily limit is 25000 dollars. Also worth to mention that if you want to withdraw Cryptocurrency, your daily limit is 50000 dollars.

Same as with other crypto trading platforms, you must get authorized, to get started on Kraken, which has taken me a week; however I have heard that some people have to wait longer than that.

The interface is very friendly, and there are some excellent charts too; however the security is that I want to point out again. Two-factor authentication is what you want to use. Meaning, you will use your password as well your Google authentication using google authenticator. This is what you have to set up, as the system will not do it for you.

You must have a smart phone, and you must download google authenticator, is a free application, then set it up for better security.

I have covered all those online trading sites I have used previously, and those are all legeit genuine websites.

There are many more online trading platforms that are also legit; however, I have not tried them out yet; therefore I can not review them.

All through, you may find other websites through coinmarketcap.com, and they all should be legit.

Still, you should do some more research and make sure that you are comfortable using any cryptocurrency trading site.

Chapter 14 - Be aware of scammers!

As I mentioned previously, there is a huge industry around Bitcoin and other cryptocurrencies. Still, many people just beginning of learning about Bitcoin, and most of them who does, want to buy some. Unfortunately, I have to tell you that hackers are one of the worse enemies when it comes to Bitcoin.

Hackers can hit anytime, at anyone, and they can steal Bitcoin from personal accounts, as well from large online trading companies.

Even experienced people do get hacked time to time, and the reality is that most people are only taking security seriously once they got hacked.

It's nice to own some Bitcoin for weeks, then months, and keep on buying more and more, however, if you do not take extra security measurements, one day you might wake up, for your wallet being emptied out.

Any purchase you have, you must make sure that you use a hardware wallet and save all your values on it. Still, my number one recommendation is Ledger Nano S:

https://www.ledgerwallet.com/r/e101

I can not emphasize enough, that authorities, such as police or even your bank, will not be able to help you once you get hacked.

There are some trading platforms who might get hacked and will repay you in full, such as Bitfinex did. However, there is no guarantee that they will do it again, in case history will repeat itself.

Now that's being said, as I mentioned there are many new comers to this industry, and beginners who are often having no knowledge, they hear that the value of Bitcoin has been increased dramatically; therefore they quickly want to get some.

Anytime when you or anyone you know is so excited, and want to rush to the market to buy some Bitcoin, please do not do it, and those you know, tell them that is one of the worse things they can do.

Sure thing, you hear that Bitcoin is a good investment, and you have money to invest, so let's do it right? WRONG!

There are so many scammers around the web, that is very difficult to say which ones are legit, especially for those, that are novice to this market.

Once you have the experience, you will know how people with bad intentions are trying to scam people, using Ponzi schemes and other methods. How do they reach potential victims?

Well, they go where the people are. Those might be Facebook, Twitter, or youtube, and begin advertise themselves.

Trying to make you believe, they will give you a huge profit margin or even make you a millionaire. They are using techniques such as creating a fake facebook account, or youtube channel, as well counterfeit websites.

First of all, anytime you hear things like double your money or making a profit every day, even if Bitcoin market is down, there is something dodgy going on.

Unfortunately, there are many people losing thousands of dollars because they fall for some of these scammers or thieves, and there is not much they can do about it.

Let's begin with some examples as facebooks, and twitter comments.

Scam No 1.

To increase you Bitcoin investments, you can start trading today with only 10 Bitcoin, and earn up to 30 Bitcoin in less than a month...

> adams kristen 19 hours ago
> use binary options to increase your bitcoin investments you can start trading today with only 10btc and earn up to 30btc in less than a month,for this reason many bitcoin owners are now opting to use binary options to improve their bitcoin investments as much as possible,many people have suffered from the stress involved in investing,many investments takes long revenue to mature or earn viable revenue,binary options comes with short term payout unlike the traditional formats...this is an opportunity for those that have lost too much and those that are tired of earning less,inbox me for more details kristenadams52@gmail.com

There is no point reading this any further, however, let's get the first sentence right.

So if I invest <u>only 10 Bitcoin today</u>, that is currently around 45000 dollars, <u>I can earn 30 Bitcoin in less than 30 days</u>.

So basically in 30 days, I could make 135000 dollars right? Wow!

That's sounds good! In fact, it sounds too good to be true! That would come to 4500 dollars daily profit.

This is obviously a scam. I am not even going to ask how much he or she is making in this business model, simply because there is no point, so look at another example.

Scam No 2.

Anyone need Bitcoin is very cheap rate so please Whatsapp me my number...

> Arvind Roy 1 day ago
> Anyone need bitcoin is very cheap rate so please Whatsapp me my number (9451972146)

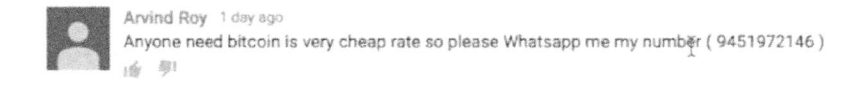

Right! So anything like this, you ever see, <u>do not send a text message</u> at all.
There is an enormous hacking industry going around stealing people's phone numbers, then trying to use your number to their advantage.

Scam No 3.

Cloud mining – click on the link, free start, payout after ten days.

> Goog Gooog 3 days ago
> Cloud mining https://goo.gl/BpvXfG Free start, payout after 10 days.

OK, so there are many different kinds of cloud mining; however even some are real such as Genesis mining or Minergate; still, I wouldn't click on links that I am unsure of it.

I am using Minergate, and my friend is using Genesis mining; however, I can not recommend others as I don't know any other legit company.

However, if you want to mine some Bitcoin or another cryptocurrency, you can use Minergate for free. (more on this in the bonus chapter)

https://minergate.com/a/f5dccb84d2696 b16a1c8bced

Another famous mining facility is called Genesis Mining, however this is not free to use, and it is not you but them who mining for you:

https://www.genesis-mining.com/

Scam No 4

Onecoin scam. Onecoin has been introduced as a new cryptocurrency; however, it has turned out to be the biggest scam in the crypto world.

Unfortunately, many people have lost their life savings, due to investing into this fake currency. Those individuals who have been promoting this currency, have been sent to jail already in India as well in Dubai.

ONECOIN
STATE OF THE NATION

The company has formed in Bulgaria with the intention of hoping to find gullible people around the world and sell them, making them believe that one day, they all become rich.

The problem is that you can only buy Onecoin from the distributors, however once you are ready to sell it, you will not be able to do so.

They will not repurchase it from you, and if you think that you can find an online exchange, you are wrong.

No one dealing with this, therefore it has no value. As I mentioned before coinmarketcap.com is where you can find all crypto currencies, however, you will not be able to find Onecoin there.

How do people fall for Onecoin? Onecoin was promoted as a possible next Bitcoin, also seen adverts where they have advertised Onecoin and Bitcoin in the same sentence.

This, of course, cought some people's attention, and begin to purchase it.

However, once they have realized that it has never made it any further, people wanted to sell it, but it was too late.

Please avoid investing in any new currency that you can not find on coinmarketcap.com.

Scam No 5

<u>New-age-bank scam.</u> This website has been shut down for a while now, however at the beginning of this year was active, and many people have fallen for their scam system.

What they have been promoting, is that if you invest 0.05 Bitcoin, they will return you 0.1 Bitcoin in 30 days, however, if you spend 1 Bitcoin, they will return 2 Bitcoin in 28 Days.

Of course, if you invest 5 Bitcoin, they would return 10 Bitcoin in 24 days. The VIP package is where you would spend 10 Bitcoin, and you would get returned 20 Bitcoin but this time in 23 days.

So, basically, thay will double your money either way, however more Bitconi you send them, faster the doubling it will be.

Now, this is sound too good to be true, so please anything like that, you must avoid.

All through their websites are now shut down. Still, there were hundreds of people who claimed that were scammed, while they have been operated.

The reality is that I could go on and on about these sites, so let's look at some common issues they all have.

Scam alert No1:

They put pictures of famous people on the website. However, you can not find out exactly who is the CEO, or the link to About Us does not work, or worse there isn't one.

There are some occasions where the Contact Us menu option isn't working or once again there isn't one on the site.

Scam alert No2:

Unreasonable high return. Anyone who claims that can double or triple your money is 99% scam. In the crypto world, no one can tell you exactly what the market will bring us.

Of course, it is possible to double or even triple your money, however, if someone guarantees that for you, that is possibly a scam.

The value of Bitcoin has increased since January 2017 from 900 dollars to 4500 dollars by the end of August 2017.

It is true. However there is no guarantee for that to happen in the next year, even I really would like that to happen, it might not going to.

Scam alert No3:

Unsure the purpose of the company. Sometimes if you can click on the About Us menu option (if it works), and you find that you are not 100% clear what the company does exactly, that could mean a possible scam.

Some might say, that they are trading for you, but then how do they make up for their profit? Well if you can contact the company, you should ask them questions like:

- What is the company does exactly?
- How do they guarantee my investment?
- How do they ensure security?

If you get a response that is a bit wishy-washy, well then probably is a scam. If they don't even reply to you, then again, it is possibly a scam.

Scam alert No4:

The particular coin is not listed on coinmarketplace.com. If you can not find a coin that you are interested in coinmarketcap, then you should probably turn around and run away from that coin, as its probably another scam.

If there is a new cryptocurrency, do not go to their own website and start investing. First you should always check coinmarketcap.com, simple as that.

Scam Alert No5:

The coin is centralized. I have explained this before on Volume 1 Blockchain book, that once a system is centralized, it is controlled by an individual or a company.

If it has a central Server, that can be monitored; there is no guaranty that they will not go and alter it or to make any changes.

Again, I could go on and on about possible scams, as well how to recognize them, however, if you are a newbie, you might find it useful that, there is a dedicated website for Bitcoin scammers, called:

<u>http://behindmlm.com/</u>

This site is a collection of possible scams, where also people reply to one another, explaining experiences, of different websites.

Again, please be extra vigilant, and research on any trading company before you would invest into it. Double check their site and make sure everything works, as well checks out ok.

Also if you can contact them, then by all means do so, and ask questions that might concern you.

Genuine company should get back to you within 24 hours due to time differences, and they would provide you with an answer that you were looking for.

Chapter 15 – Bitcoin Trading

I have explained previously how to find genuine cryptocurrency trading platforms, however I have never got on the topic of trading with Bitcoin.

The reality is that I am not a Bitcoin trader, all through I do make some moves here and there, still, my belief on trading is not something that is beneficial for long term business, as it comes with lots of stress as well a huge risk.

I do believe in Bockchain, and Bitcoin too, as a technology. Once you have enough knowledge of how the technology works, and what issues it has, that require fixing, you can predict changes in it's value.

Of course there are other occasions too, besides it's technology features, when it comes to its value and that is fame.

For example, this year the value of Bitcoin was 1700 dollars, however when Wannacry ransomware has hit worldwide, by an anonymous hacker group, they have asked for ransom to be paid in Bitcoin.

Within a week, the price of Bitcoin has gone up to 2400 dollars. Ransomware has hit more then 150 countries, by disabling the logon functions on more then 200,000 computers worldwide. It is important to note on that incident that Wannacry has not reached to individuals, instead Hospitals and government agencies, as well Police stations. Some speculate that many organizations have invested heavily into Bitcoin, in case another attack happens, so they could pay up the ransom right away.

All through it makes sense, others including me, also believe that is a side effect of Bitcoin made it to the news once again. It has been learned in previous years, that each time Bitcoin was in the news, there is an enormous amount of people who began to take interests about it's nature.

Those they do so, usually take it a bit further and realize the potentials, than start to invest into Bitcoin. What also have been learned that each time when the market capitalization grows, parallel the value of Bitcoin grows too.

Having said that, if you can follow the news of Bitcoin, your odds of trading with Bitcoin, are certainly will increase. I have researched a historical data for Bitcoin, and I have compared the market capitalization to the value of Bitcoin.

The date is from coinmarketcap.com, and if you click on this link, it should take you there too:

https://coinmarketcap.com/currencies/bitcoin/historical-data/?start=20130428&end=20170828

In case you don't feel like going through years of data, I have taken some notes for easier understanding what has happened over the years.

Please note that coinmarketcap only generated a report since 2013; therefore I wasn't able to get earlier figures.

However, I believe that only looking at the data of 2017, can be useful already. I have followed the market capitalization, followed by the date and the value of Bitcoin, upwards until recent dates.

Market Cap	1 BTC in US $	Date
1,500,520,000	135.98	Apr 28, 2013
870,912,000	80	Jul 08, 2013
1,547,640,000	140.89	Aug 31, 2013
3,129,190,000	304.17	Nov 07, 2013
5,029,340,000	437.89	Nov 15, 2013
11,124,900,000	1001.96	Nov 27, 2013
5,583,670,000	443.37	Apr 10, 2014
2,853,930,000	211.73	Jan 17, 2015
10,511,900,000	716	Jun 13, 2016
15,667,900,000	989.11	Feb 01, 2017
20,253,700,000	1280.31	Mar 03, 2017
25,133,100,000	1618.03	May 05, 2017
30,999,000,000	2004.52	May 19, 2017
40,817,100,000	2581.91	Jun 03, 2017
46,276,200,000	2899.33	Aug 04, 2017
47,778,200,000	3290.01	Aug 05, 2017
53,720,900,000	3293.29	Aug 06, 2017
60,242,100,000	3949.92	Aug 12, 2017
71,425,500,000	4455.97	Aug 15, 2017
71,809,200,000	4416.59	Aug 27, 2017

As you can see, it has taken years to reach 10 billion US dollars in market capitalization, however alone this year, since January, Bitcoin has reached 70 Billion in market capitalization alone.

Not to mention the other hundreds of Cryptocurrencies, totalling 159 Billion. Meaning

Bitcoin has only 45.1% dominance of the whole market.

Why am I telling you this? Well, because the value of Bitcoin has reached an amount that we have never experienced with any other currency, there is a tremendous volatility that comes with it.

Meaning, there are days when the value of Bitcoin goes up and down in hundreds of dollars, but for better understanding, let me show you an example of today.

I have taken a screenshot of today's Bitcoin charts, and I can see that today morning at 6am the value of Bitcoin has gone down to 4224 dollars, however later on at 5:44 pm the value has reached 4385 dollars. That's 161 dollars difference.

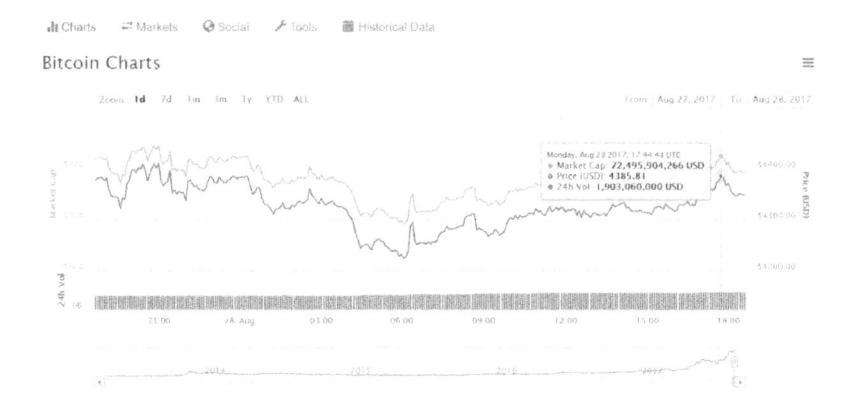

Please bare in mind that crypto market is a free market, open 24/7. Meaning you can sell, buy, exchange anytime you wish, from anywhere in the world.

There is no need for waiting until 9 am for the traders to open, neither the banks until Monday, in case of Saturday night you wish to sell some Bitcoin.

The 161 dollars difference over 1 Bitcoin it's a huge difference. However, if you think that is practically unfeasible to trade with, then you might wait for another day or two, and make a sale than.

Many people have left the traditional trading using fiat currencies and precious metals, so they learn and invest learning the crypto world instead. If you do have 10K worth of Bitcoin, and know your way around the crypto market, you can make 100-500 dollars a day, only trading with Bitcoin. Believe me, many people's new full-time job is to trade online, using Bitcoin as well other cryptocurrencies.

I am providing some facts on historical data, however, I have to mention that I am not a financial advisor, and please don't take these as financial advice.

Also, make sure that you understand, that if you choose to invest into Bitcoin, or other cryptocurrencies, this is a very high-risk market, and you should not invest more then what you are willing to lose.

As I mentioned, the crypto market is very volatile, therefore if you want to utilize the market volatility, you probably thinking like a trader. Investors, on the other hand, buy Bitcoin and hold on to it for weeks, months, even years to come.

What you can do, is this: You can become a mixture of both, an investor and trader blended together.

What I mean is that, instead of holding onto all your Bitcoin, and get angry at your self why didn't you sell it and bought more, try to take another approach. Lets imagine that you have

200 dollars worth of Bitcoin. What you can do is hold on to 100 dollars worth, and do not touch it whatsoever, even the market goes up or down.

This makes you an investor. The other 100 dollars worth of Bitcoin, sell it when you think the market is right for it, then wait until the market goes down again, and buy it back for cheaper.

This is the risky part of course. For example if you look at the historical data I have collected, you can see that the value of Bitcoin has gone deep down as 211 dollars in January 2015.

This event has made people believe that the time of Bitcoin has reached the end.

Even many people, who have bought Bitcoin previously for as much as 1000 dollars, they have sold their Bitcoin as they thought that Bitcoin will sink completely.

However, those who kept hold of it for years to come, has become wealthy.

Bonus Chapter - Bitcoin mining with laptop

Many people get confused on the topic of Bitcoin mining, so let me lay it down once again. Bitcoin mining is a process of turning computer power into Bitcoin.

It allows you to generate Bitcoin, without the need to actually buy them. In case you heard about mining already, you might also heard that Bitcoin mining is impossible, using your home computer.

This is somewhat true however, there are other ways to go about mining with your laptop, or even with your Android mobile phone. Mining Bitcoin back in the day was relatively simple.

All you needed is a laptop or a desktop PC, and if you have mined Bitcoin, it might taken a day or two to generate one full Bitcoin. People used their home computer by utilizing its CPU power.

This is also known as CPU mining. However, over the time the hashing rate has been increased, therefore CPU mining has become impossible.

Next, people began to use their gaming PC-s, using graphical cards instead of their CPU-s, and that was somewhat profitable for a while.

This method is called GPU mining, however, as I just mentioned GPU mining became very difficult too.

The Next level of Bitcoin mining was done by ASIC mining machines. ASIC stands for Application-Specific Integrated Circuit.

These machines have been built for one purpose only, and that is Bitcoin mining.

Nowadays the hashing power has been so difficult, that even with the latest and greatest

ASIC mining machines are very difficult to mine Bitcoin. Imagine that having an ASIC mining rig that costs you around 2500 dollars, you could probably be able to mine a whole Bitcoin in every 2-3 months.

However, this is an average figure, as you might not be able to mine your first Bitcoin just in 5-6 months time.

Due to this reason, solo miners have began to create mining pools, were all single miners are able to participate their mining power.

Together are always able to mine Bitcoin, and they can also generate some additional Bitcoin by the transaction fees.

This could generate them on an average of 100 to 200 dollars a week.

Considering that these latest and greatest ASIC mining rigs will be exhausted within 2-3 years, it's a better profit then becoming a solo miner, and wait for your luck.

In case you are more like a miner type then an investor, and you don't want to invest either, in Bitcoin or expensive ASIC mining machines, I have a nice surprise for you.

Having an old laptop might be just enough for you to start generating your Bitcoin.

What you have to understand, is that any computer can mine Bitcoin, even it's old, and the CPU is not up to date, it will do the Job.

You will need to have a computer, a software called Minergate, and of course an internet access.

Minergate is available to be accessed on the following link:

https://minergate.com/a/f5dccb84d2696b16a1c8bced

Before you download the Minergate software, let me explain that using this software can be very demanding regarding using your computers CPU or GPU.

However, the good news is that you can set it up in the way, that it would never use more than 10-20 % of your CPU.

Once you ready to download the software, just click on the option called downloads.

Here you can choose what operating system you have on your laptop or computer, then just go ahead and download that software.

All available GUI solutions

Windows	Mac	Ubuntu	Fedora
7 or later 64 bit Minergate v6.9	10.9 or later 64 bit Minergate v6.9	14.xx & 15.xx 64 bit Minergate v6.9	23 or later 64 bit Minergate v6.9
7 or later 32 bit Minergate v5.19		16.04 or later 64 bit Minergate v6.9 Up to 60% more effective in Ethereum mining	

Archive

Win 64	Win 32	Mac
6.8 7 or later 64 bit	–	6.8 10.9 or later 64 bit
6.6 7 or later 64 bit	–	6.6 10.9 or later 64 bit
6.5 7 or later 64 bit	–	6.5 10.9 or later 64 bit

To download the app to your smart phone, you have to go to Google Play Store, and search for the App called Minergate.

After a successful download, you can start to mine many different kinds of cryptocurrencies, and the beauty of this is that you can convert them all into Bitcoin.

Of course, it is optional, as you might want to keep the coins for yourself, and turn them into Bitcoin a later day, but it's completely up to you.

Minergate supports the following currencies:

- Z cash
- Ethereum
- Ethereum Classic
- Bitcoin
- Litecoin
- Bytecoin
- Monero
- FantomCoin
- QuazarCoin
- DigitalNote
- MonetaVerde
- Dashcoin
- AEON
- Infinium-8

Once you download the Minergate App and software to your computer, you have to register by providing your e-mail address, and password. Then, once you are ready to mine, you can only start by opening the software. Another great thing is that you can use multiple machines at the same time, and use them all as your miners. For example, I use two mobile phones, as well three laptops to mine mostly Monero. Monero, is a good choice, as its also supported on the mobile App. On your mobile phone, you can also make some adjustments, such as: do not mine when your battery is low, or only mine when it's connected to a WIFI.

I use both options, and it is great as once I am near to an access point, and my phone is authenticated to the local WIFI, the App starts up automatically. Once you open the software on your desktop, you can navigate to the menu options and click on view. Here you can tick or untick those currencies that you want to see or mine:

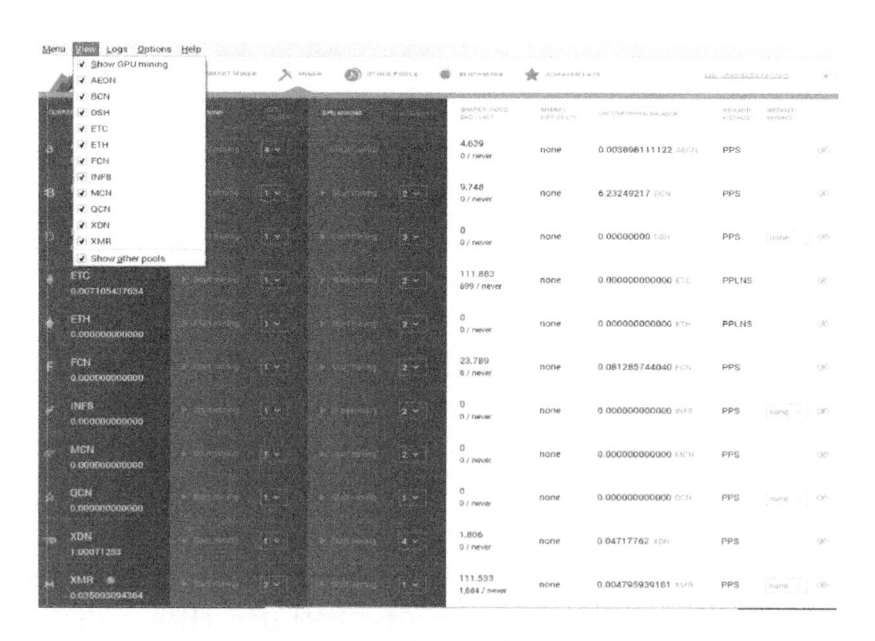

You can also click on smart mining, that will start automatically extract the coin that is the most profitable, which in most cases are Monero. By the way, Monero is currently worth 132 dollars and keep on rising.

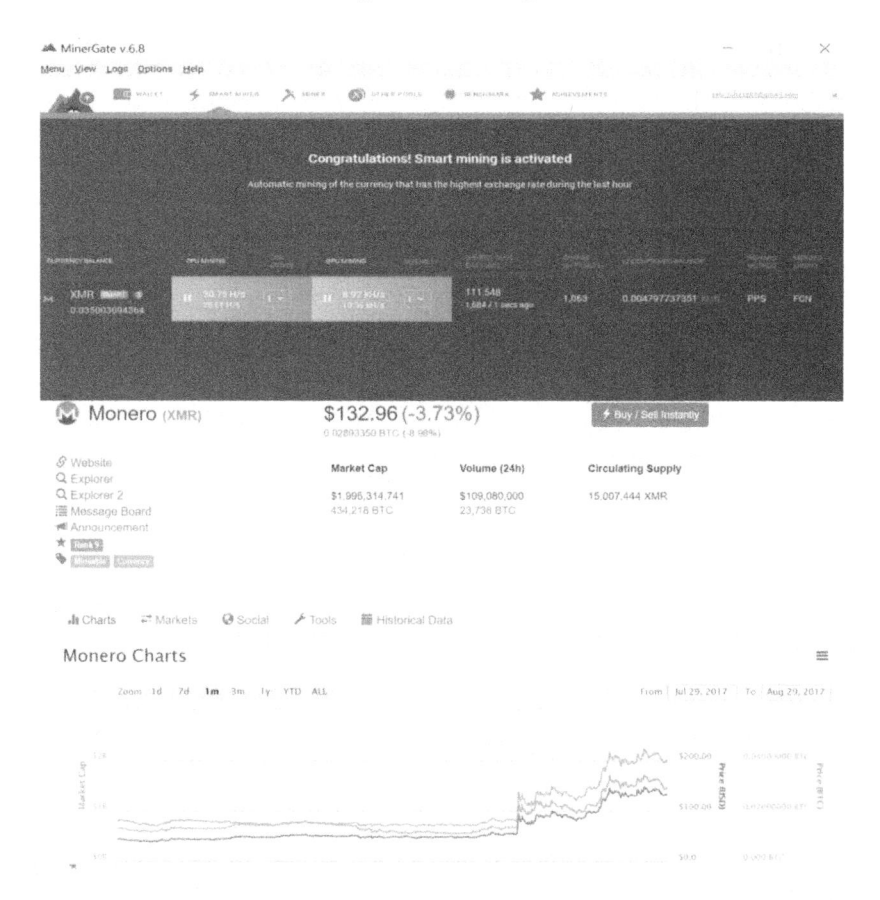

Additionally to the miner function and smart miners, you have free wallets to use for each of the cryptocurrency you mine. All the conis that you are capable of mining with Minergate, can be converted into Bitcoin, but as I mentioned, it is not necessary. Another function that Minergate has is the achievements section, where you receive different performance Prizes for the style of your mining.

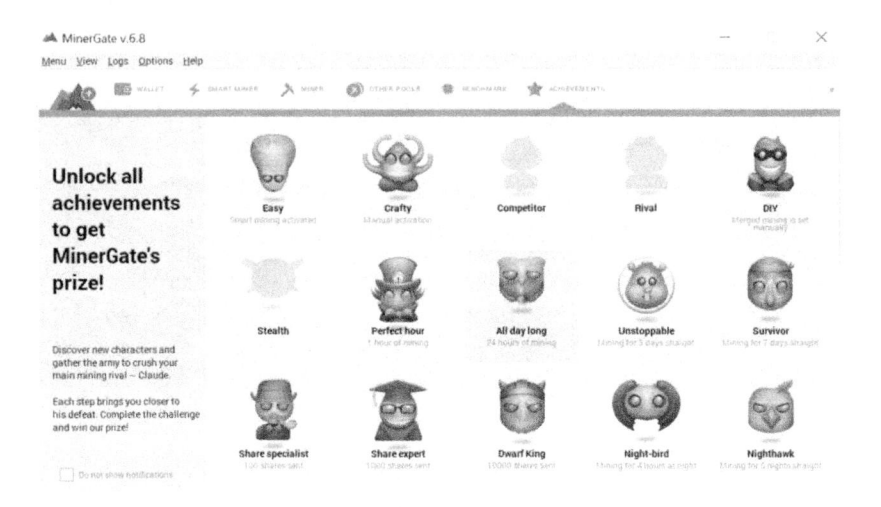

This is of course only for fun. However, it's a nice gesture from the creators. I will be honest with you, and let you know, that the smart miner all through picks up the most profitable cryptocurrency; however, it is not always true. The reality is that even other coins are not that lucrative.

Still, you might be able to mine more because everyone is mining Monero. I have realized that mining other currencies, you might get a better hashing power that would increase your mining capabilities, therefore not always Monero is the most successful, instead other coins, that fewer people are mining.

Again to start with Minergate, just follow this link:

https://minergate.com/a/f5dccb84d2696b16a1c8bced

Being honest, Minergate will not make you rich; however an average laptop can generate you around 5 to 10 dollars a month, and if you can use more than one laptop like I do, as well mobile devices, such as phones, or tablets, you can generate more profit.

Another issue is the electricity bill. If you live somewhere, where the electricity bill is very cheap or even free, that's great; however, you have to understand that once you start mining, your computer will require more power. Therefore it will consume more electricity than usual.

Either way, I hope you will try it out and will like it too, as this is one of the fastest, and easiest way to start mining and generating your Bitcoin.

Conclusion

Thank you for purchasing this book. I hope the content has provided some insights into what is really behind the curtains when it comes to the future of money.

I have tried to favour every reader by avoiding technical terms on how to invest in Bitcoin. However, as I mentioned few times, to fully understand how Bitcoin works, you may choose to read two of my other books on Blockchain as well on Bitcoin Blueprint.

Volume 1 – Blockchain – Beginners Guide
Volume 2 – Blockchain – Advanced Guide
Volume 1 – Bitcoin Blueprint

The Blockchain books are focusing on the underlying platform of Bitcoin, the technology called Blockchain.

Blockchain Volume 1, is for beginners; however, Volume 2 is very technical. Still, I did my best to use everyday English, and making sure that everyone can understand each of the technologies and their importance.

Bitcoin blueprint focuses on Bitcoin for beginners; however, I have fitted some interesting topics around the future of payments, using reputation systems with Bitcoin-Blockchain technology.

My upcoming book on Bitcoin, will provide more details on Bitcoin mining, profitability, and what exactly miners do.

How miners are often trying to manipulate the market, what techniques they use, and how they try to control mining pools, using super expensive ASIC mining hardware.

I will provide information and secrets on Chinese Bitcoin miners, as well their exclusively produced ASIC mining rigs, that no other miners capable of using.
Lastly, if you enjoyed the book, please take some time to share your thoughts by post a review. It would be highly appreciated!

Made in the USA
Las Vegas, NV
26 February 2021